GROW YOUR OWN LEADERS

ex libris

Richard A. Soar

GROW YOUR OWN LEADERS

A practical guide to training in the local church

Anton Baumohl

Scripture Union
130 City Road, London EC1V 2NJ

© 1987 Anton Baumohl

First published 1987
Scripture Union, 130 City Road, London EC1V 2NJ

ISBN 0 86201 481 6

Phototypeset by Wyvern Typesetting Limited, Bristol

Printed and bound in Great Britain by Cox and Wyman Ltd, Reading

Contents

Index to Case Studies

Acknowledgements

The material in this book and the thinking behind it have arisen from Scripture Union's involvement in training over the past twenty years – twenty years that have seen rapid developments from the training of children's workers to training in a broad range of ministries including the training of trainers themselves. Over the past six years Scripture Union's Training Unit has explored and developed a theory and practice of training geared to the needs of the local church. This experience has shown that training does not have to be mechanistic, dull and threatening but can be exciting and fun, leading participants into new and exciting ways of serving the God who calls all to be involved in his mission on earth.

I would like to thank all those who have pioneered training in Scripture Union and in the church and who have contributed, perhaps unknowingly, to this book: all past trainers and associates of SU's Training Unit, Joan King, Margaret Old, Andy Stanton and the late Jim Punton; those who kindly read the early manuscript – Colin Matthews, David Pitts, Arkle Bell, Marlene Cohen, John Grayston, Trevor Lloyd, Geoff Ovens, and Pauline Bell. Thanks to Jill, my wife, who attempted to learn how to use the word processor in order to get the manuscript typed and patiently reverted to the typewriter when that training course was cancelled for the third time. Also thanks to the Rising Sun at Pensford where some of the earlier writing was carried out in peace away from the telephones.

The house group leader's job description and material on apprenticeship was taken with permission from earlier work done by Pauline Bell, Scripture Union's Training Officer in the East Region.

How to Use This Book

What picture does the word 'training' conjure up in your mind? Lion tamers, dog handlers, football coaches, driving instructors, college buildings? All these images seem so remote from the life of the local church. But training is increasingly on the agenda of the Christian community. Unfortunately those traditional views of training sometimes persist, creating a resistance amongst those who feel that training in the church shouldn't be quite so mechanical. In other instances the term is seen simply as a contemporary replacement for the traditional teaching activities of the church.

Grow Your Own Leaders has been written as a practical guide for Christians who wish to train those with various responsibilities in their church or organization. It provides both a basis for understanding the purpose and role of training, and a range of training ideas that can be put into practice. It has been written in the belief that training has an important part to play in every fellowship and Christian organization.

The range of suggestions that have been offered for developing training should cater for a wide range of situations – the small rural church, the inner city church, the church on the housing estate and the large suburban church. Where the church as a whole is not ready to introduce training schemes the ideas can be adapted by groups within the church. If, say, only the youth leaders, Sunday school teachers or pastoral team members are enthusiastic, *Grow Your Own Leaders* can help them develop training schemes suitable for them alone. There is also help for *individuals* who want to be trained (see chapters 4 and 5) whether they come from churches struggling to find leaders or are the only people involved in their area of ministry in larger churches.

Throughout the book there are examples and case studies. These are often set in very specific situations, recognizable as common areas of work within the church. They can be applied to training in work inside *and outside the local church community*. They are designed to make the ideas and suggestions more concrete. They should be treated as illustrations and not models of perfect practice. Where lists are provided these are not meant to be exhaustive. All are offered as catalysts to encourage the reader to think about their own situation – where they don't fit your church or your thinking be prepared to adapt and develop them so that they are more appropriate for you.

In any Christian book words are a minefield. Words like leader, discipling, and training mean different things to different people. Where appropriate these words have been defined, elsewhere their definition should be clear from the context in which they are used. Such words as ministry, service, job, task, and role are used interchangeably to refer to the wide range of activities that could benefit from training. I have not felt it worthwhile to enter into any theological exploration of these words as some might like. On occasions words have been culled directly from industry and management – words such as 'on-the-job', 'supervision', 'distance training', 'trainee'. This has been to save time and lengthy explanations – hopefully they will not carry with them all their industrial connotations.

If you are new to the idea of training, or find that the ideas explored in this book are beyond anything that you have ever considered before, do not be put off. Be prepared to select a few ideas and to try them out. Here's one way to use this book:

1. Skim though all the chapters keeping your current situation and immediate needs in the forefront of your mind.
2. Identify anything that appears to fit your current situation and immediate needs and read it a second time more thoroughly.
3. Don't bite off more than you can chew. Start with training on a small scale – with a pilot group or using a sample method. If your trial run works with one group or individual, try it with others, and explore further training ideas.

Don't be afraid to be selective and to experiment, trying out different ideas until you find one that works for you and for your situation.

If you are ready to develop a coherent strategy for training in your church or group, work through the book more thoroughly and systematically. Chapters 1–3 provide a theoretical framework to help you in your thinking. Chapters 4–6 offer four means of training which you can adapt and use in various combinations. Chapters 7–9 offer help for those who will take responsibility for the training. If you want to

train your own trainers you may need to look to
outside agencies offering this service.

The questions after each chapter and the training
audit in Appendix A are designed to help you relate
the material in the book to your own church or group.
They could be used as a study course for the deacons,
eldership team, any group of leaders, or individuals
who want to plan for training.

Finally a word of caution. Training isn't the answer
to the failings and struggles of the local church. It is
one means of helping Christians in their discipleship.
It must always be seen in the broader context of the
church's life and work.

1
Does the church need training?

Stuffed in the back of every seat in Bath Road Church you will find the duplicated weekly newsheet. Its first page gives a clue to the importance the church places on the weekly rounds of events and activities that it announces.

```
                        Bath Road Church

Sunday      10.45 am    Children's church and creche
            11.00 am    Morning service (with the music group)
             6.30 pm    Evening service (featuring the drama group)
             7.45 pm    Under 30's group
Monday       7.30 pm    House-to-house visiting begins
             8.00 pm    Music group practice
Tuesday      7.15 pm    Church council meets (followed by separate
                        meetings of the pastoral team and sidesmen)
Wednesday    7.45 pm    Home group meetings for study and prayer
Thursday     2.30 pm    Mother and toddler group
                        Women's fellowship
Friday      12.30 pm    Pensioners' lunch club
             7.00 pm    Junior youth club
Saturday     7.30 pm    Senior youth club
```

Bath Road may not be like your church and indeed may not be typical at all. Your church may boast more activities or considerably fewer. Bath Road is certainly not cited because it represents the ideal that all should strive for! It is simply there to illustrate the level of responsibility given to unpaid, untrained, volunteer leaders and the increasing need and desire to rely on 'ordinary' church members for the maintenance, functioning and growth of the church. Creche helpers and Sunday school teachers look after the Christian nurture needs of the children; committees and their chairmen share in the responsibility for management and decision-making; youth leaders play a vital role in helping adolescents to cope with their own development, the Christian faith and integration into the church family; the leaders of the pensioners' lunch club and the mother and toddler group may spearhead the links between church and the local community; the pastoral team help to share the burden of providing counsel and pastoral support for those with particular needs; many have important responsibility in enabling adults to learn and grow as disciples.

These 'ordinary' church members are referred to as 'lay leaders' in some denominations and although this term is not universally acceptable we will use it as convenient shorthand for the duration of this chapter

CHANGING ATTITUDES

The past twenty years have seen significant changes at Bath Road Church. At one time all activities were tightly controlled by the minister. He took responsibility for teaching, pastoral work, administration, worship and outreach. He initiated and controlled and was a faithful product of his own training. Not only did he accept this situation but the fellowship expected it!

Today the same church views the intolerable physical and emotional burden of 'one-man ministry' as unacceptable. Leadership and responsibility are now shared and a variety of lay people are involved in a variety of roles. What is more the current minister and the members of the church find this partnership a desirable means of furthering God's work in their community.

This changing role of the minister and growing involvement of lay people is a common trend. It can be witnessed across the denominations and, to some extent, throughout the world. It has sprung partly from a change in the understanding of the role of the minister and partly from a shortage of trained 'professionals' in particular denominations. But the increasing reliance on the laity is not only a result of practical pressures. Alongside the need to share the workload has been a theological awakening. There has been a gradual rediscovery of the church as a community, a body and a family. These are biblical concepts that suggest co-operation, the sharing of tasks and people working together.

Together with this acceptance of lay involvement in the local church has come the recognition that the lay person's involvement in the local community is also an expression of ministry. Involvement in the street community, at the children's school, in local politics, at work, in the home etc., is now recognized as part of the Christian's responsibility, a means of sharing in God's mission on earth.

Following on the heels of new attitudes to lay involvement have come changes in attitudes to training. At one time training was only deemed necessary for the full-time professional. The cost and time required to prepare someone for a multi-functional role was accepted. Gradually it has become clear that the part-time volunteer can also benefit from training.

The church's desire to encourage lay training may have been influenced by changing trends in society, where there has also been an increasing role for the volunteer. Volunteers are active in large numbers in the youth service, with counselling agencies, and in community-based projects. People who offer their services in this way are often required to undergo training before they are finally 'let loose' on the public. Training is also now more readily available through courses run by local government and other specialist training agencies.

An increasing number of training courses and packages are also available for those with responsibility in the local church. Courses may be timed to fit in with the volunteer's home and work life and designed to meet their specific needs. The increasing availability of these training resources stems in part from a growing demand from lay leaders themselves. When John takes over the youth work he recognizes his need for help in arranging programmes and handling relationship problems. Sally, the new Sunday school superintendent, wants to be effective as she 'enables' the team of teachers in their work. Jane and Brian want to know how to foster pastoral care in their new home group. As these people recognize their need so they look around for help.

Despite these positive signs there is no room for complacency. While many accept the principles of shared leadership and lay involvement, they may still operate as if only one person has the ability and authority to do the work. Although many applaud the value of training it never actually occurs. There exists a noticeable gap between theory and practice. The reasons for this may be complex but could include:

a) underlying feelings of insecurity in both ministers and lay people.

b) lack of resources, people, money, time or materials.

c) not knowing where to begin and how to change the existing system.

d) not knowing how to turn the learning into practice.

e) lack of clear understanding of the nature and purpose of training and a confusion over the different roles of training and teaching.

At present where training does occur it is often outside the orbit of the local church. Courses may, for example, be run at regional or national levels by denominational and independent agencies. These involve sending people away for days or weekends. People come back with varying responses: some are enthusiastic and encouraged, others feel frustrated that their particular needs haven't been met. For some a sense of hopelessness develops a month or so after returning when they see their new vision, skills and ideas rejected by others in their church. Many return feeling that their training is now complete and that their work as counsellor, teacher or play group leader has some professional stamp of approval.

The time has come to begin to develop a coherent rationale for training in the local church. A rationale that helps define more clearly what training actually is; that sees it as an essential part of discipling and mission, integrated into other church activities; and that recognizes training as a continuous process that requires planning over periods of time and is not accomplished through one-off events. This rationale should also form a basis for defining the role of trainers and identifying the skills needed to train others.

TRAINING – SOME BIBLICAL INSIGHTS

Jesus was not only an outstanding teacher; he was also an accomplished trainer. He trained the disciples in preparation for the various activities in which they were soon to become involved. Jesus' training style involved a form of apprenticeship where the disciples watched as he worked before being sent out to have a go for themselves. Imagine how the disciples felt as they went out on their first solo run (Luke 9: 1–6, 10). They had heard the theory and seen it work in practice, they were even aware of some of the potential problems and opposition – and now they were being sent out on their own. Imagine their return. What mixed feelings they would share with Jesus – the exhilaration of having accomplished a worthwhile task, the sense of failure over experiences of rejection or tasks unfinished, the relief at getting back to a secure environment. In today's jargon that important meeting with Jesus recorded in verse 10 would probably be called a 'debrief' or 'supervisory session'!

There are many occasions in the Gospels when the disciples were present to observe Jesus fulfilling his ministry – healing, teaching, handling confrontation, answering tricky questions, discerning and meeting needs. On other occasions he selected a handful of disciples to accompany him – as if he wished them to observe more closely the things he did. After many experiences, Jesus offered a special word of explanation to the disciples as a means of enhancing their understanding. Three elements can be identified in Jesus' apprenticeship training.

OBSERVATION → EXPLANATION → INVOLVEMENT

This apprenticeship lasted the three years of Jesus' public ministry and then the disciples were, in one respect, on their own – 'articles' completed but still learning and developing as they got on with the task. Some would restrict their understanding of training to this one biblical example but however valid this means of training remains it is not meant to be our sole method today. Neither is it the only biblical rationale for training in the local church.

The New Testament as a whole paints a very detailed picture of the nature of discipleship. It is portrayed as allegiance and commitment, as learning and growth, as work and service. Training brings together two of these elements – service and learning.

Disciples are called to *serve* God, share the good news of Jesus with others and to 'go and make disciples'. They are called to be involved with God in his mission of renewing the whole of creation – not passively but in an active way.

Disciples are also *learners* in the same way that the early disciples were learners. Discipleship itself is a process of growth into maturity. This can also be viewed as a renewing process, whereby God's people are gradually restored to the image of their creator – the image in which mankind was made.

Alongside these pictures the Bible indicates the means by which service and learning will be achieved. Not by the independent efforts of people or sole actions of God but by partnership – God and his people working together.

From creation itself mankind has been called to work with God in order to fulfil his purposes on earth. This partnership recognizes both the supernatural work of the Holy Spirit – initiating, enlightening, equipping, changing and completing – and the efforts of Christians to learn and to serve to the best of their abilities.

The idea of a joint relationship also applies to the work of helping other disciples to serve and to grow. In our training we must recognize and accept both the work of God's Spirit and our own efforts and skills as trainers.

So often in helping disciples to grow, the church has majored almost totally on their growth in understanding and in holiness. People have been helped to understand the great truths of the faith, to wrestle with the mysteries of the nature and purposes of God. Through worship, they have been encouraged to reach out and respond to God. If anything has been neglected it has been the practical help that people need to serve God in whatever way he calls them. If they can grow in their understanding and in spirituality then surely they can grow in their *ability* to serve God.

Linked to these ideas of discipleship is Paul's image of the body to describe the Christian church community. One means, according to Paul, by which body-life is maintained is through the utilization of the gifts given to each member – gifts for service, gifts to help in the growth and building up of the body. Discipleship is not a private affair; it is experienced and worked out in the context of a community in which co-operation and teamwork are important to the vitality of the whole. In the twentieth-century version of the local church community there are numerous gifts, talents and skills which are required to help the community to function and grow. These include what are sometimes called (unhelpfully I believe) the 'spiritual' gifts of healing, discerning, speaking in tongues, prophesying, etc. There are also the 'educational' gifts of teaching, pastoring, evangelism and the 'practical' gifts of administration, hospitality. All are from God, given to the individual in one way or another, and all require discipline and training in their use.

This biblical picture could be developed further by examining the Paul/Timothy relationship as a model of training and by considering the early church's understanding and use of leadership. These themes must be pursued by the reader alone, however. It is sufficient for our purposes to suggest that there is enough biblical evidence to encourage the church to consider training for service as one of its functions running alongside all the other 'activities' with which it is involved.

At this point it's important for us to keep a sense of perspective and to remind ourselves that discipling and the Christian community are not just about service. Some feel that many of our churches are excessively activity-orientated and could quite easily become dominated by training events which prepare people for the various responsibilities and tasks.

Discipleship has a strong *'being'* as well as *'doing'* element to it – it's about *living* as Christians as much as it is about service, it's about *enjoying* a relationship as much as it's about growth and work. In a book that focuses on training it might be understandable if the reader felt that training was being raised on a pedestal above everything else that takes place. That certainly isn't the intention.

It has already been pointed out that much of the training that does take place is initiated outside the local church. A variety of agencies run courses, and these are well attended. Many of those who attend are motivated to do so by the local church, who see the value of equipping those with responsibility in this way. In other cases it is simply an individual who, finding nothing to cater for his or her needs in their own fellowship, takes the initiative and looks outside.

The time has come for the local church to take more responsibility for the training of its own leaders, and for training to become an integral part of its function. Here are six reasons for returning this responsibility to the local church:

1. Training for service is an integral part of being a Christian disciple. If the local Christian community is the primary context in which discipling takes place training should be on the agenda. Failure to integrate training in this way prevents many from seeing it as part of their discipleship. When Jim and Irene are sent away to a training course on house group leadership they could be forgiven for getting the idea that training is an optional extra or a luxury the church struggles to afford.

2. The context for service is the local church. Training is not an end in itself – it is a means to helping people be more able to serve or minister in some way. But this service will have a specific context. If training is to be useful it must help individuals function within

the actual situations in which they find themselves. As this context will usually be the local church and surrounding community, the most effective training will be that designed with a specific context in mind. Briar Baptist Church has its own way of organizing and running its house groups, Sunday schools, evangelism, pastoral care etc. and training must help the leaders at Briar to develop the skills to work in their peculiar situations. The same is true of the rural parish, the ecumenical project on the new housing estate and the inner city mission hall. So often people from these backgrounds who attend external courses find it hard to relate what they learn to their situation.

3. Many jobs require training over a period of time. A Sunday school teacher does not learn all there is to know after attending a day conference; their training needs to continue throughout their time as Sunday school teachers. There is always something new to learn: skills to develop, problems to solve, weaknesses to work at. Only the local church can plan and sustain training for those with responsibility over a period of time.

4. Leadership is continually changing. The rapid turnover in lay leadership in any local fellowship demands a continuous search for new leaders. People move away, retire, die, run out of steam, or move on to some other area of responsibility. Only the local church can ensure that the stream of people taking on new responsibilities are adequately equipped to start their new task.

5. The various training needs of the church will need to be co-ordinated. There is a growing demand from Christians for training but many of these people have other jobs and responsibilities. They don't want and couldn't manage time away in a college or even on

a short course. They want to know how to chair their committee more effectively; to build better relationships with difficult teenagers; to communicate the good news more effectively to their old people or children; to counsel those with problems; to lead the worship with more confidence; to enable their home group in discussion. The motivation to have their needs met will soon evaporate if the means aren't readily available. As the needs and demands grow it becomes essential that the most effective use is made of time and resources. The church has to take on a co-ordinating role, being continually alive to the needs that exist, and matching them to the means.

6. The local church provides an environment of mutual support and encouragement. Training by its very nature encourages people to review, evaluate, change and develop. It can be a 'stretching', stressful experience for some. The ideal environment for training is one of security and support, where changes that need to be made can be shared, prayed over and implemented with the help and understanding of others. This conducive atmosphere is most likely to be experienced in the local expression of the body of Christ.

After several discipline problems in the youth club the leader attends a training event on 'Relating to Adults'. This highlights major weaknesses in her own relationships with the young people. She becomes aware of major changes she needs to make. Only with the understanding and support of others in her fellowship is she able to begin to work things out back in the club.

CATALYST AND CO-ORDINATOR

If the local church is to take its training role seriously it must fulfil two important functions. Firstly, it must act as a *catalyst*, encouraging, motivating and inspiring lay leaders in their development: helping Peter whose talents have lain dormant to see that he has something to offer, discerning that Mary has the gift of helping others in need, encouraging Joan with tremendous artistic potential to prepare for a role in the life of the church. As a catalyst the church can actively encourage people to acquire and develop skills. In order to do this there has to be a clear understanding of what training is and why it is important. This understanding must be shared by leaders and members alike. In some churches there will be the need to start with some clear biblical teaching on the value of training for the lay ministry. In others the fact that training is available may be the starting point. All churches require a knowledge of the different means of training and how to match these with the different needs that they have. An atmosphere has to be created where training is both acceptable and important, and an activity in which people want to participate.

The second role is that of *co-ordinator*: bringing together training needs and the means for meeting them. The needs have to be identified, for example:

- training for those who are new to a job
- training for those involved in teamwork
- programmes that offer development to people who have been in the same role for a number of years
- training that refreshes and renews those who have been in the same role for a number of years

• 'first aid' training to meet an immediate need or problem.

The means of meeting the training needs have to be identified:

• courses offered by training agencies, denominational training services, colleges, etc.

• training schemes the local church can offer itself, using its own resources

• training materials in the form of books, packages, etc.

In its role as co-ordinator, the local church will have to find the blend between providing the training itself and using resources from outside the church. Co-ordinating will also mean being aware of the range of training that is needed by the group or groups in the church and relating this to (i) the time that can be allocated, (ii) the motivation and availability of those to be trained, and (iii) the skills/expertise available to carry out the training.

The rural or inner city church that doesn't enjoy a high level of lay involvement in leadership or just doesn't have the same membership as a suburban church may not have sufficient demand for training, nor the time or skill to mount its own programme and may look outside for almost all its training needs to be met. Whatever its size, it is unlikely that any one local church can meet all its own training needs. It may join with others in its locality (or use current denominational groupings such as deaneries, circuits or fraternals), invite outsiders to help specific groups, or send people on external training courses. This will probably be as well as undertaking some degree of training by using members of its own fellowship as trainers. The key role of the church as co-ordinator of training is to devise some form of plan that shows how, when, where training will take place and for whom.

Where is your church or group in relation to lay leadership and training? What current attitudes and practices can you identify? To help you, here are some common attitudes that exist in churches. Which fits your church? You may clearly fit one description or want to mix a cocktail with parts taken from a number.

The unaware
- 'Training? Isn't that what happens in industry and business?'
- 'We've never considered it as having a role in the church.'
- 'We've always seen the church's purpose as worship, teaching and outreach.'

The uninterested
- 'We haven't got time for training. We've more important things to do.'
- 'We're not professional.'
- 'It's the minister's job to take the major responsibility, that's what he's paid for.'
- 'We don't want to supplant the minister's authority.'

The professionals
- 'We're taking training on board.'
- 'John and Jean have responsibility for our training programmes.'
- 'We expect everyone who takes on responsibility to be trained.'
- 'We want the work of the church to be professional

and effective rather than amateurish and lacking in impact.'

● 'We have budgeted for training – time and money.'

The threatened

● 'I'm the one with the responsibility and the authority, it's not appropriate to share this with the laity.'

● 'They can get on with the day-to-day running of groups but I must retain ultimate control.'

● 'Training would create totally wrong expectations and encourage the laity to take initiatives that are not appropriate.'

● 'I've seen the hassles that churches get into when they train lay leaders.'

● 'I spent three years at college. It would be wasted if I allowed volunteers to take over leadership.'

The career-planners

● 'We have a variety of training programmes running regularly.'

● 'People are encouraged to train for something they seem to have a gift or talent for.'

● 'Those involved in leading any of our activities are required to train. Others can opt for any training session – it may not be useful in this church but they may be able to use it at some future date if they move elsewhere.'

The trend-followers

● 'It's a good thing, training. The growing churches are doing it.'

● 'We don't fully understand what it is but we mention it a lot and put on the occasional course.'

● 'We wouldn't stop anyone from going on training courses elsewhere.'

The interested

- 'It's high on our agenda to think about.'
- 'When other things are sorted out we will think about training.'
- 'We'd train people – if we had people!'

The self-sufficient

- 'We don't need training – training's rather man-centred and mechanistic.'
- 'Living in the Spirit provides all the training anyone could ever require.'

The overstretched

- 'We already have twenty-three meetings each week. We couldn't squeeze another activity in!'
- 'We couldn't expect people to turn out again. Those who would attend are already over-committed.'

The overwhelmed

- 'Training? Wonderful, but where would we fit it in?'
- 'A great idea, but where on earth do you start?'
- 'We're still grappling with church growth, home groups and improving the family service. Perhaps when we've sorted them out.'

Attitudes to training can be deeply ingrained and are often a stumbling block to change. Negative attitudes may be held by church members, the church minister or elders, or by both. Changing such feelings is a major task. The first step is to be aware of people's attitudes – not to assume or imagine negative feelings but to check what people really think and feel. Step two involves trying to understand why people feel the way they do. Some may be threatened at the possibility of losing their power:

'Training may make him more skilful than I am and I may lose my position and influence.'

Others may be concerned at the thought of learning new things:

'I've learnt how to do it over the years and I don't need to change what I do. It works perfectly well.'

There may simply be a lack of understanding and experience of training:

'We've never had to train people before, why start now?'

The third step is to be clear what changes in practice and attitudes you wish to see. The final step is to communicate these changes in a way that helps even the most insecure to give them a go. It obviously isn't always as simple as it sounds but the ability to consider change with care is an important principle to keep in mind when going through this book.

THINGS TO DO

1. Carry out some surveys in your church.
   a) Discover people's attitudes to lay involvement in leadership and to the role of the minister (full-time professional) in the life of the church.
   b) Discover what people understand by the word 'training' in the context of church life.
2. Explore the picture of training that evolves in the Bible.
3. Use the section 'Identifying yourself' in this chapter to identify your church's present attitude to training. Make this the basis for discussion in house groups, the church's council meeting, etc.

2
What is
Training?

The word **training** is used in different churches to describe different activities. One church describes a *sermon series* as 'discipleship training'. In another a *guest speaker* is invited to talk to the house group leaders. A third church uses a *training pack* with worksheets and visual aids, produced by a respected Christian organization.

Training means different things to different people. Such diversity of definition may be one reason why so many churches are vague about their training role. One cause of confusion may stem from the failure to distinguish training from the more general teaching and educational activities in the church. By limiting our definition of training it may be possible for the church to focus its attention on a much neglected area of its work.

For the purpose of this book training is defined as those activities that help equip people to carry out a particular task or take on some specific responsibility. The special emphasis in training is enabling people to discover *how* to do something. Training, therefore, is related to very specifically defined activities or jobs - chairing a committee, working with children, counselling, welcoming newcomers, working in the church office, door-to-door visiting, etc. All these responsibilities could be called ministries or areas of service. Training provides one means by which the gifts, talents and skills of Christians are developed to fulfil their calling.

The words 'teaching' and 'education' have much broader meanings and in the church are associated with the general support and nurture of Christian disciples. Training with its specialist meaning becomes *one* element of education and discipling, taking its place alongside all the others.

With this limited definition we can see that each of the three activities described at the start of this chapter may have a part to play in providing training, but of themselves probably don't go far enough to ensure that people know *how* to do what they are being invited, or called, to do.

Having considered in general terms the confusion that exists in the church's understanding of training, let us now turn to examining some major emphases in more detail and from these attempt a more detailed philosophy of training for the local church.

A VARIETY OF APPROACHES TO TRAINING

In churches where training is recognized as the means of helping people fulfil a particular ministry or area of service the approach to training will often have a particular emphasis or flavour. Four of the most popular approaches are:

1. *The Bible-centred approach* stems from a concern to explore the biblical principles for carrying out any work in the church. Participants are encouraged to

look at biblical texts which may be expounded by a teacher or studied together in small groups. Under this method the training of counsellors, for example, might focus on incidents in the life of Christ – how he handled people who came to him with problems. The case studies from the Gospels are used to extract principles which participants are encouraged to apply to their own work.

2. *An issue-based approach* focuses on the main issues encountered in a particular job or ministry. The issues may be explored in a variety of ways: by bringing in an expert, through discussion and sharing of participants' own experiences, or using film or video. This is a way of training from real-life situations that actually confront the trainee. Again taking the example of counsellor training, this approach would involve looking at the nature of drug abuse, marriage breakdown, or adolescence, defining the issues and considering how to handle them in appropriate ways. In training Sunday school teachers, issues of discipline, integrating church and Sunday school, the place of the family in Christian nurture and the theology of childhood might be offered in an issue-based approach.

3. *Skills training* begins with an analysis of the job in terms of the skills needed to do it. It encourages participants to practise the skills both away from the job and in the early stages of doing the job. The counsellor would be encouraged to practise and develop the skills of listening, clarifying, questioning, confronting and problem-solving. The house group leader may be trained in programme planning, running a discussion, identifying and handling group processes. The youth leader might be trained in using audio-visual equipment, building relationships

with teenagers, programme-planning playing games, etc.

4. *Awareness training* may also be described as sensitivity training or personal growth training. This type of training works from the premise that to function better a person needs to be aware of him or herself, and sensitive to other people. It is used in training people for tasks that rely heavily on the development of quality relationships such as small group leadership or counselling. It helps participants to become more aware of how they feel about themselves and how they see themselves. It also helps participants to be more sensitive to how others are feeling and behaving. The thinking behind this approach is that the new personal awareness will improve the way people relate and communicate with others.

The counsellor's sensitivity to others is critical. He or she must learn to identify the feelings being expressed behind the words of another, and to be more aware of how their own words affect the person they are counselling. Those on welcome duty are able to put themselves in the shoes of a newcomer to the church and understand their feelings of strangeness. The hospital visitor learns to be more sensitive to the sick person being visited.

A VARIETY OF STYLES OF TRAINING

With the variety of approaches goes a variety of styles:

1. *Expert-centred training* places an expert at the centre of the training. Many training events are staffed by people with expertise and proven 'success' in a particular field. This can suggest that there is one

particular way of doing the job for which people are being trained. Unfortunately, those with proven experience and ability may not be able to communicate what they do and how they do it to others. Some experts may be poor at communicating their experiences to others. Many have problems in remembering how the novice feels and may be unable to help those whose background and gifts they don't fully understand.

2. *Programme-centred training* places a programme or method at the centre of the training. There are an increasing number of packaged training courses available to local churches. To the busy church they may be very attractive and may have a tremendous amount to offer. Most of these programmes are taken and used wholesale without any adapting. The needs of the local situation and the people involved can become secondary to the material covered by the training programme.

3. *Participant-centred training* places the people being trained at the centre of the training. The trainer attempts to discover the needs of those being trained and to address these needs in the training offered. This training style demands a high level of participant involvement. The trainer will be much less dominant. In some types of participant-centred training the trainer simply becomes the servant of the group, taking on a completely non-directive role.

A VARIETY OF CONTEXTS FOR TRAINING

Training is carried out in a number of contexts. Here we will focus briefly on three. Each will be covered in more detail in later chapters of this book.

1. *Training on-the-job*. One unhealthy form of this training is 'throwing people in at the deep end'. There are a number of much healthier ways of training people while they are actually involved in the task or job they are being asked to do. The use of supervision and apprenticeship training are both explored in chapter 4.

2. *Training at a distance*. This is simply self-training without the help of a trainer – about the only way to train when there are no training courses or trainers available. It might include the use of books, programmed learning texts, computers, videos etc. and is the focus of chapter 5 of this book.

3. *Training off-the-job*. This would usually involve attending a training course run for any period of time from one evening to a full three years at a residential college. Courses may be run by the local church for its own members, or by other agencies unrelated to the church from which participants come. See chapter 6 for more details.

TOWARDS A TRAINING RATIONALE FOR THE LOCAL CHURCH

How do we evaluate these different approaches to and styles of training? Which is the most appropriate context for training? The strength of training will lie in the way these variations are combined into a satisfying whole. Jesus' training of the disciples was, in the same way, an integrated approach which brought together a number of the elements we have just looked at.

A practical approach
Biblical principles and models need to form a

foundation for any training in the church. The Bible can help us to:

- understand the role and purpose of the various ministries and tasks in the church
- identify some of the training needs
- evaluate training methods to ensure that they are consistent with Christian values.

It is important, however, that we don't restrict our leaders to the confines of Bible times and to ways of working that are inappropriate to our situations. It is, for example, good when training Sunday school teachers to look at Jesus' teaching methods – but sad if this means neglecting the possibilities of video, overhead projector or simulation games in helping children learn. Training that relies totally on biblical exposition and Bible study may help people to understand something of what their role is and why they are involved in it. But a totally different approach is needed to help them develop the skills they need.

Biblical knowledge and principles can be carefully integrated into the programme by the trainer. Here are some examples:

i) In identifying training needs for would-be counsellors the trainer includes something on the biblical teaching about salvation, which emphasizes God's concern for our 'wholeness' and 'health'.

ii) In planning a session on building relationships with children a trainer uses, as a starting point, Jesus' attitude to children as expressed in the Gospels and leads from a short Bible study into an exercise that encourages people to reflect on their own experience of children.

iii) In choosing a human relations exercise (see chapter 6) as one method of helping a group of counsellors to learn about themselves and others, a trainer is guided by the fact that it reflects Christian values in its assumptions about people and the importance of open and honest relationships.

This process of integrating biblical principles into training ensures that there is time to give to the practical elements of training.

We can develop our understanding of training by reflecting on both the Bible and our experience of life and work today, and by bringing the results of these two lines of thought together.

A focus on **issues** shows a concern for the real situations that face people involved in ministry and is an essential part of a training event. But it is important to distinguish between exploring the issues and developing the skills to tackle them. Issues-based training that leaves little or no time to develop appropriate skills can also lose its practical value as training. Issues are usually best addressed as they arise and begin to confront people in their work. Someone starting out as a member of the pastoral team may benefit more by attending a course in basic helping skills than taking part in a discussion on the factors that cause marriage breakdown, or the effects of child abuse on adolescents.

It is the practical approach offered by **skills and awareness training** that has, so far, been neglected by the church. To develop a more integrated approach it will be necessary to give more time to the practice of skills and the development of greater sensitivity, possibly at the expense of the issues-based and biblical approaches. Skills training is still mainly associated with industry and very little has filtered into the church – in fact rarely are roles within the church identified in terms of specific skills. Awareness and sensitivity training on the other hand are often associated with the boom in humanistic psychology and popular therapies of the 60s and 70s and are shunned by some as being non-Christian and dangerous. Both are fundamental to the act of training (and help to distinguish it from teaching). One difficulty here concerns the fact that biblical principles and issues can to some extent be taught by someone with teaching gifts. Skills and awareness training require different skills. They are the domain of the *trainer*. The church is relatively well-equipped with teachers but on the whole theological colleges do not equip students to be trainers. The skills of the trainer are explored in chapter 7.

In summary, an integrated approach to training will produce a practical emphasis in helping people to develop skills and awareness. This is not to neglect either a concern for biblical principles or an exploration of issues, but neither of these approaches on their own should be seen as adequate in helping leaders know *how* to fulfil their responsibilities.

The importance of people

Training begins with people and the task. So often, outside speakers are invited to address topics, or programmes are drawn up, that bear no relation to the needs of the people being trained. These packages are often excellent at explaining what the job is about, at giving tips, at offering ideas and providing inspiration. They are not always good at equipping people to do the job.

Training must focus on the local situation and especially on the people being trained. It is important to keep in mind that training is concerned to help people carry out a task that God has given *them*, and to which *they* are being called. This requires understanding where they are in terms of their experience, knowledge and skills so that the training will move them on in their development. Training also needs to take account of the local situation – of which an outside speaker or training package will not be aware.

But training is more than just helping people to carry out a task. It is part of the discipling process which helps them to grow into the people God desires. In this respect it must be sensitive to their needs and strengths and failings as well as to their vision.

Training often achieves more than equipping people for work and responsibility. It can also:

i) increase people's understanding of their ministry/ service and its relationship to the church

ii) fuel a vision and enthusiasm for that work

iii) contribute to the wholeness (health) and growth of those involved

iv) be an agent of change and enable people to adapt to the changes going on around them

v) lead to the church's more effective engagement in God's mission.

Training that starts with experts and packages rather than people will often fail as an effective discipling tool.

A choice of contexts
Each of the three contexts for training outlined above, has a part to play in training people in the local church. Training on the job gives people first-hand experience and can provide some of the most thorough learning. Off-the-job training allows people space to work at things without pressure. Distance training has a flexibility that can help meet some of the more obscure training needs. Ideally the context can be chosen to suit the particular needs of the individuals or groups

being trained and the situation that exists in the local church. Where churches can provide a variety of training experiences they will be able to cater for most of the training needs that arise.

In conclusion, as we begin to integrate the various elements above we begin to see the emergence of a model of training that:

i) places an emphasis on skills and practice: helps people to know *how* to do the job but does not neglect biblical principles and addresses major issues

ii) demonstrates a concern for people and is a servant of those who are called rather than dictating to them and restricting their God-given ministry.

CASE STUDY 1:
A training philosophy

Scripture Union's Training Unit has been developing a philosophy of training over the period of its existence. Below is a statement of some of the values and assumptions that underlie this philosophy. It is used here as an illustration rather than a model.

1. Training is concerned with enabling people to fulfil a task or role as part of their God-given ministry.
2. Training in its methodology and content should be in accordance with biblical principles and values.
3. Training is one means that the Holy Spirit uses to equip and empower people for God's mission.
4. Training is concerned with the needs of the participant as well as the needs of the job.
5. Training starts from where people are in terms of experience, skills and understanding in order to move them on so that they are more able to carry out their work.
6. Training is concerned to preserve the uniqueness of the individual. Each person brings something unique to the work they do because of the image of God in them and the

special gifts and abilities they have been given. The trainer is not a perfect model of how the job should be done.

7. Training recognizes the process by which adults learn and the problems they have and is designed to help adults learn in appropriate ways. For more on this see *Making Adult Disciples* by Anton Baumohl (Scripture Union, 1984).

8. Training is essentially a practical process with real concern for skills and awareness as well as knowledge, understanding and attitudes.

9. Training is often a long-term process and can have a role to play in the development of an individual throughout his or her life.

10. Training involves keeping the correct tension between meeting the needs perceived by the people being trained and meeting those perceived by the trainer – when these are different.

11. Training necessitates the use of a wide range of methods to enable the learning process to take place.

12. The trainer acts as an enabler, combining a variety of skills in directive and non-directive approaches.

TRAINING HEALTH WARNING

A final note of caution: training creates expectations in people. If you embark on a training programme for your church, be ready for the consequences.

1. You will create the expectation that there is a role for the trained person to play. Is that true or will they have to wait until the next house group leader leaves? If you are really preparing people for a role in another Christian community somewhere it will help them to know this from the start.

2. You may convince existing leaders that the work

they are doing isn't really for them, that they are not called or gifted. A training event may be a place where leaders are lost. Are you prepared to lose people from particular areas of work? Can you help these same people find some form of involvement more suited to their talents?

THINGS TO DO

1. In a paragraph, try to sum up your church's understanding of and approach to training.
2. Identify any changes you would want to make in your training as a result of reading this chapter.
3. If you already have a well developed training ministry in your church write down the values and assumptions behind that training (see Case Study 1 as an example).

3
Preparing the way for Training

Like all well run activities, training benefits from careful thought and thorough preparation. There are a number of important questions to ask before jumping on the training bandwagon and insisting that everyone in the church attends a training course. Does the church have the leaders it needs? How do you decide who to train? What do people feel about 'being trained'? How do you decide what to include in the training? This chapter begins to address these questions in order to provide a foundation on which to build the church's training. If posing these questions of the whole church is too big a task then they could be asked of any area of church life – the house groups, the women's work, the Sunday school etc.

PREPARING GOD'S PEOPLE FOR TRAINING

1. Attitudes to involvement
A major assumption throughout this book is that there are people in the church to be trained. In many churches and church groups there is a real dearth of lay leadership. The perennial headache is encouraging

people to take responsibility for activities or to fill vacant posts. Many fellowships rely on the faithful few who take the strain of leadership and as a result suffer the effects of overload. Churches in rural areas and around our city centres often have small congregations and few members who accept a role in leading aspects of church life. There isn't the time or space to address this issue in any depth here, all we can do is list some of the strategies that have been developed to encourage people to take on responsibility.

a) *Major teaching programmes.* Some churches use existing teaching channels such as the Sunday sermon or midweek meeting to encourage people to use their gifts, consider the implications of shared leadership, explore the relationship between discipleship and service, and accept their responsibility in God's mission on earth. Regular teaching on such topics can help to create positive expectations towards involvement in the work of the church and, coupled with the opportunity to sample various activities, can help people to identify how they would like to get involved.

b) *Special focus.* A week's (or month's) special focus on the church's various activities can bring leadership needs to the attention of the church. This could be linked with other themes such as stewardship or mission. During the week there might be opportunity for people to hear and see what happens at various church activities, to be given insights into what leadership or involvement might mean and to have the chance to sample some activities.

c) *Gifts surveys.* Every member of the Christian community is encouraged to identify the contribution he or she could make. These surveys often use questionnaires or group study material that help people to think about themselves – their strengths, abilities, skills, experiences and interests – and to consider how they might be utilized within the church.

d) *Sample training week*. A range of short training courses are held to give people a taste of some area of ministry. Churches have offered these during mid-week meetings, as an alternative to other study/ fellowship groups. They may be spread over four to six weeks and people opt for one area of ministry that they would like to explore with no obligations once the course has finished. One church offered a choice from working with children, pastoral skills, catering in the church, visiting the sick and elderly, preaching and leading worship.

e) *Church induction schemes*. Similar to (d) above, these give people a taste of various areas of church life before they commit themselves – a visit to the youth club, Sunday school, catering group meeting, etc.

f) *Broaden horizons*. Help people to see their involve-ment in the local community as part of ministry. God calls many to service outside the local church at work, at home, in local politics, community work and so on. To broaden people's view of ministry may help many to see that they are already involved in God's work without realizing it. Carry out a survey, offer teaching on ministry outside the local church, prepare discus-sion material for groups, invite those who already recognize the validity of their ministry in the world to speak to church groups.

g) *Limited 'contracts'*. So that people don't feel they are taking on a job that will last into eternity, groups have explored the use of limited contracts for all positions of responsibility. A job can become a millstone around a person's neck. With little prospect of anyone else taking over, guilt replaces vision and any sense of calling. People could be invited to join the old people's lunch club team for two years; worship leaders can see a natural and honourable way of moving on when their four-year contract comes to an end.

h) *Personal invitation*. People approached personally may be more open to accepting responsibility than if a general appeal for volunteers is made. This should provide an opportunity for the person being invited to look at the nature of the job and its implications for their current routine.

2. *Attitudes to leadership*

There are churches which readily accept the notion of training for leadership but who define leadership in a very limited way. They will restrict training to the few in prominent positions – those who teach, or the decision-makers and the pastors. Training has something to offer *all* Christians involved in some area of service or with a job to do in the local church or surrounding community.

If we accept Paul's model of the church described in Ephesians 4, we see the potential for everyone being involved in some way and everyone having an important part to play in the growth and development of the whole. This may require some change in attitudes to leadership and responsibility in the church. When using the word 'leadership' in this book we are referring to anyone with some responsibility or job in the church. They may be a recognized leader (eg house group leader), a member of a team (eg Sunday school teacher), or someone who gets on with a job quietly on their own (eg church cleaner). Some areas of church leadership may be temporary or short-lived (eg

houseparty planner, outing organizer, evangelistic
campaign co-ordinator); others may be long-term.

All of these people can benefit from training.
Training will vary according to the nature and extent
of the responsibility. Some people involved in short-
term and routine jobs may need no more training than
a short verbal instruction; others – especially those
involved in working with people – will require longer
training spread over a period of time, and some will
benefit from training at various stages throughout
their involvement in a particular ministry.

In many areas of church life the value of shared
leadership is recognized because the task is too big for
one person. Where this is the case there is a real benefit
in treating those involved in the same area of ministry
as a team – the youth work team, the eldership team,
the Sunday school team, the team of visitors. Teamwork can be a microcosm of the 'body' image of the
church in that there is shared vision and the exercising
of complementary gifts and skills. A team has an
advantage over the lone leader in that it offers those
involved:

  – mutual support from others who know and
    understand the stresses and strains
  – encouragement and motivation
  – greater strength and resources brought to the task
  – greater commitment through team cohesion
  – a sense of value and purpose as the team is
    identified as such.

Training teams together helps to strengthen the team
and its work and can be an important way of
encouraging people to attend training events. Training can also focus on teamwork skills so that the team
becomes a more effective *team* as well as the individuals being better equipped to fulfil their ministry. A

sample training programme on teamwork is included in Appendix C at the back of this book.

3. *Attitudes to training*

Training can be a very demotivating word for some adults. They may associate it with early unpleasant experiences during their work life, feel it's something only for the young, consider it too time-consuming, equate it with involvement and action, see it as involving change and having to do something new. Those who find reading difficult or who aren't skilled in using words may feel that it is only for the 'educated'. A more detailed examination of the fears that adults often experience when confronted by learning can be found in chapter 4 of *Making Adult Disciples* (Scripture Union). There are a number of things that can be done to allay some of the fears and to help Christian adults accept training as a valid and important activity for the local church community and for themselves.

a) *Explain the importance of training*. This involves setting the scene or creating the right climate for training. It can be done in whatever way best communicates to the fellowship as a whole – through a letter, teaching sessions, sermons, team meetings etc. People need to be helped to understand:

  i) the link between training and discipleship and between discipleship and growing in our ability to serve God (see chapter 1).
 ii) that Christian adults have some responsibility for their own growth and development. This includes looking at their own lives in order to identify the skills, knowledge and attitudes that they need for any roles they take on.
iii) what training is.

Setting the climate cannot be achieved once and for all by addressing the topic through one sermon. It needs to be seen to be part of the life of the fellowship, and is achieved through regular communication of one form or another.

b) *Provide the means*. Talking about training will be a waste of time unless training is actually offered. Certain people in the church could, for example, act as reference points – collecting information about courses and disseminating it to all concerned. Or the church might run a regular training programme every year to cater for the major training needs. It may be appropriate to train one or more people to be trainers and to fulfil a training ministry within the fellowship. If the opportunity to be trained is on hand, people are more likely to take advantage of it.

c) *Incorporate training into the job*. When those being invited to take on a task are informed about the nature of their role, make it clear that it includes a training element. The new member of the visiting team will know, for example, that her work includes attending a training event on at least three evenings a year; the new member of the worship team accepts a commitment to one training day a year, and so on. If you have job descriptions for any of the jobs in your church, include training and personal development on the list of major tasks. In this way training becomes integral and essential rather than optional and an afterthought. Having a limited 'contract' (see p. 48) for a post may help people to feel that their commitment – including the training involved – is reasonable, and that if their personal circumstances change there is a time when this commitment can be reconsidered.

d) *Involve people in the planning*. Adults will be more committed to training if they feel that they have had a part to play in the planning. Consult the youth team about the content of a training event for them. Consult the participants about how long a training event might last, and where and when it might be held. It could be helpful to provide an opportunity for those who will be trained for the first time to talk openly about their feelings at the prospect. This will give them a chance to share their fears, feelings and fantasies. A personal invitation can also be a great motivator to anyone who might not readily get involved even if they have been consulted about the content. Everyone you want to attend could receive a personal letter, phone call, or face-to-face invitation.

e) *Plan training realistically*. Remember that members of the fellowship have other commitments and responsibilities. A full-time three year training course for children's workers in the church may be what you would like to offer – but you have to be satisfied with covering the important elements in three days spread over the year. It can help if you try to put some training into existing meetings rather than create something new. A training element could be incorporated into the drama group's fortnightly practice or the counsellors' weekly prayer meeting. Where training is new to a group try offering a short sampler course which fits into the time people have available. This kind of experience can help people to cope with training and to develop more positive attitudes. Where training involves extra meetings or events, attendance at other regular church meetings could perhaps be played down, especially for those whose diaries are already full. Training events could be run in parallel with other regular church activities – an evening for sidesmen coinciding with the church's regular midweek meeting, for instance. Whenever training is planned it needs to be communicated to those attending as early as possible so that it doesn't clash with their other commitments.

f) *Communicate clearly.* As well as explaining when training is going to take place it is important to explain what is going to happen. Give people details of what topics are to be covered, what will be expected of participants, how long the training will last. It can also be helpful to explain the course objectives, ie what you hope people will gain by going through the training. In Case Study 2 the objectives for a training course are laid out so that those attending will know what to expect.

CASE STUDY 2:
The training objectives of a training course

. . . at the end of this day event for playgroup leaders participants should:

- have an increased understanding of the world of the under-five
- know how to plan a two-hour playgroup programme
- understand the place of play in the under-five's learning and growth
- have an opportunity to share problems they have faced
- know how to use one of the following activities with under-fives: finger play, movement, sand and water activities, storytelling.

---

g) *Use the power of teamwork.* Training a team of leaders together can help people to feel less threatened and may even be a means of putting a little positive pressure on people to attend.

h) *Do not impose too great a demand on people.* Training should not take people out of their depth. A good maxim is to start where the participants are and aim to move them on, stretching them just enough to help them develop in their work. Use methods that non-readers and those who are less articulate can participate in and enjoy.

i) *Make the training interesting, relevant and enjoyable.* It is important to make sure the training really addresses the needs that people have or the skills, information and attitudes that they require for the work they will do. At the end of any training it should be clear how what has been learned relates to the real situation people will find themselves in.

It is also important that training is a good experience – friendly, warm, fun, and enjoyable for those who participate. At the end of their training people should feel encouraged rather than overwhelmed or inadequate. This depends on a good design and the skills of the trainer. Finally it helps if people can see how the work they are doing (and therefore the training they are undertaking) fits into the life of the church or community as a whole. This broader perspective can help leaders to see the value of their work in relation to God's mission as a whole.

IDENTIFYING THOSE TO BE TRAINED

Earlier in this chapter it was suggested that anyone in the church with some responsibility could benefit from training. Here's a list of possible candidates. It isn't meant to be exhaustive!

Administrators

Bereavement counsellors

Bible study group
   leaders

Bookstall organizer

Catering team

Cleaner

Committee chairpersons

Committee members
Community projects
  team
Council members
Creche leaders and
  helpers
Dance and drama
  groups
Door-to-door visitors
Elders
Elderly people's team
Evangelistic team
Fabric group
Family service
  organizers/leaders
Flower arrangers
Gardening group
Healing ministry team
Home group leaders
Hospital visitors
Lay readers
Lesson readers
Magazine editor
Marriage preparation/
  enrichment leaders
Men's group leaders

Mother and toddler
  group helpers
Music group
Old people's visitors
Parenting course leaders
Pastoral team
Playgroup team
Political/social activists
Prayer leaders
Preachers/teachers
Sidespeople
Sunday school teachers
Visitors
Wardens
Welcome team
Women's group leaders
Workers (Christian
  dimension to office,
  factory, selling,
  management,
  housework etc.)
Worship leaders
Young people's
  fellowship leaders
Youth workers

Training can be designed to meet the needs of one of the specific groups listed above with involvement limited to a small number. There may be other times when training has something to contribute to a broad section of the church. In preparing for an evangelistic campaign, for instance, it may be important to offer a course on 'How to share your faith' to anyone in the church who wanted to attend.

On other occasions training may focus on areas

common to different activities in the church and training events may be open to people involved in different ministries. A course on 'How to use an overhead projector' might be offered to those who speak in church, youth workers, Sunday school teachers, leaders of the family service, etc. A course in listening skills might also be open to people from a range of people-caring ministries.

PLANNING THE CHURCH'S TRAINING

When the church or group has been prepared for the successful introduction of training programmes, the first real stages of planning can take place. The diagram below describes four steps in planning any training.

Diagram 1

Planning for training

1. Define the nature of the group's ministry.
↓
2. Identify the leader's role.
↓
3. Identify the key skills.
↓
4. Identify needs.

1. Defining the nature of the group's ministry
Training cannot start until it is clear what people are being trained for. This requires a clear definition of the nature of the work in which they are involved. A statement of the various objectives (or purposes) of a ministry will help to clarify what the task is to which

people are being called. Case Study 3 provides a sample list of ministry objectives.

CASE STUDY 3:
Ministry objectives

Door-to-door visiting could have completely different objectives for different groups or churches, eg:

Church 1

'The purpose of our door-to-door visiting is to distribute the church magazine, to make personal contact with every householder in the parish or district, to ensure that all are aware of church activities and to keep alert to needs that people may have which the church could meet.'

Church 2

'The objectives of our door-to-door visiting are to

i) look for openings to share the gospel with people in the locality

ii) see that everyone in the locality/parish is invited to special church family activities at least three times a year

iii) ensure the church and its work continues to have a high profile in the local community.'

In writing down objectives it is important to remember that an objective is *a specific activity described in enough detail to be able to assess whether it has been achieved to any degree at a future date*. A good way of checking that an objective is detailed enough is to ask of it, 'How will we know if this objective is being fulfilled?' Objectives should also include goals for the future – things to work towards as well as tasks for the present. This goal-setting is important if the ministry is to have any sense of direction and become more than a way of maintaining the system. The more complex the task the greater the number and variety of objectives. Pastoral work and house groups can be expected to have longer lists of objectives than the flower arrangers, church gardeners or caterers. Training is designed to fit the task. By clarifying the nature of the task the trainer and potential trainees have some indication of the training needs.

2. Identifying the leader's role

When the nature of the work has been defined in some detail the role of the leader can then be considered. One way to do this is to analyse it under three headings:

1. The knowledge (information, facts, understanding of biblical principles and models) needed to do it.

2. The attitudes/values required of anyone involved in it.

3. The skills required to carry out all the tasks involved.

CASE STUDY 4:
Analysing a house group leader's role

Knowledge
* How group fits into church life
* The purpose of his/her group
* The place of the Bible in group discussion
* How to interpret the Bible
* How small groups function
* What makes adults learn
* Biblical principles/models for using small groups
* Some basic biblical knowledge

Attitudes
* A concern for other people
* A desire to help others grow
* Appreciation of the value and importance of small groups
* A servant attitude to leadership
* Belief in shared leadership
* Enjoys preparation and planning

Skills
* Preparing a study programme
* Leading a group discussion
* Handling people in a group
* Awareness of self – strengths and weaknesses
* Sensitivity to the feelings and behaviour of others
* Communication skills
* Listening skills
* Facilitator skills

CASE STUDY 5:
Analysing a Sunday school teacher's role

Knowledge
* The characteristics of the age group
* The aims and objectives of their church
* The role of church/ family/Sunday school in helping children understand the Christian faith
* How to use the Bible with children
* Some basic biblical knowledge
* Theology of childhood

Attitudes
* A love for children
* An understanding of them
* A desire to see children understand
* A sense of fun
* A sense of humour
* Willingness to give adequate time
* Openness to learning themselves
* Commitment to the Christian faith

Skills
* Planning a lesson
* Building good relationships with children
* Using visual aids
* Storytelling
* Functioning in a team
* Awareness

The case studies above are not meant to be complete; each church will want to define its house group leaders' and Sunday school teachers' jobs in different ways, depending on how they see the particular task being fulfilled. Sometimes the distinction between knowledge, attitudes and skills isn't clear and items may be placed under more than one heading. Accurate distinctions aren't important in this analysis. What is important is to clarify in detail what the job is about as a prelude to designing the necessary training.

Looking at the two case studies above, the lists look quite daunting. It is important to remember that we can't expect people to have all that it takes to fulfil their role. They will bring some of the knowledge, attitudes and skills with them. We need to distil out the priority items in each list. Part of the job of the trainer is to help design training over a period of time to cover all the important items in that area of ministry.

As a way of helping leaders to appreciate the

priorities in their work, some churches have started producing job descriptions. A job description helps to identify the tasks involved in the work, the limits or boundaries of responsibility, and the lines of accountability. The details should link in with the purposes of the work defined (see Case Study 3 on p. 58).

Job descriptions are best discussed with the people who are being asked to take them on rather than imposed on people without any discussion. If you decide to draw up job descriptions don't forget to include *involvement in training* in the list of tasks.

CASE STUDY 6:
Job description for a house group leader

JOB TITLE: House group leader

RESPONSIBLE TO: Member of pastoral team/elder/minister

RESPONSIBLE FOR: All members of the house group

WORKING RELATIONSHIPS WITH:
1) The minister
2) Elder/member of the pastoral team
3) Other house group leaders
4) House group members

NATURE AND PURPOSE OF JOB

The house group leader's role is primarily to enable the group to function effectively. One person will not possess all the gifts necessary to ensure the successful life of a house group. The house group leader needs to be sensitive to the whole group and to the needs of the individuals in that group. The leader will then work, with God and the group members, to ensure that those needs are met.

House group leaders make an initial commitment of two years to this work, after which time their responsibilities are reviewed.

MAJOR TASKS

1. To arrange the regular fortnightly meetings and to ensure that there is appropriate hospitality.
2. To help create an accepting and caring atmosphere that encourages members to develop deeper relationships.
3. To act as a link between the leadership of the church and house group members.
4. To help people to discover their role as Christians in the church and in the wider community.
5. To encourage everyone to have an active involvement in the group. The leader has the ultimate responsibility for the pastoral care of the group even though he or she may share this task with others in the group.
6. To ensure that any group study programme is well prepared, adapted to suit the group and properly led.
7. To ensure their own continuing development as leaders by attending monthly meetings and training courses as and when arranged.

If a job description seems too formal then a simple list of duties worked out and discussed with a person taking on a new role can be equally helpful.

Together with the objectives of the ministry, the role of the leader or team member helps to define the training required for the task. The more complex the job description the greater the breadth and depth of training possibilities.

A job analysis sheet is included in the training audit found in Appendix A at the back of this book.

IDENTIFYING SKILLS

Training must place some emphasis on acquiring and developing skills. A skill is the practical ability required to do a specific task. Any task can be analysed in terms of the skills required to carry it out. Case Studies 4 and 5 offer some guidance in identifying skills. To help this analysis, four categories of skill can be identified: communication skills, human relations skills, organizational skills and mechanical skills.

Communication skills are concerned with communicating formally to large or small groups, or informally as in casual conversations. (The latter is often called interpersonal communication.) Preparing or giving a talk, using visual aids, drama and dance, mime, listening, clarifying, paraphrasing, using activity work, leading a discussion, interpreting and using non-verbal behaviour, conversation, sharing personal faith, writing, leading worship, using experiential learning and simulation games can all be classified as communication skills.

Human relations skills include: sensitivity to others, awareness of one's own behaviour, listening, questioning, confronting, handling conflict, building friendships, handling people in groups, enabling small groups to function, teambuilding, teamwork, and sensitivity to people from other backgrounds (other cultures, social backgrounds, etc.).

Organizational skills include: programme planning, preparing a Bible study, office and administrative organization, time management, organizing events.

Mechanical skills include: using an overhead projector, using a video recorder, making visual aids, playing games, operating a computer, operating printing equipment, flower arranging, building repair, plumbing, mending a fuse, working the church water heater.

It is evident that some skills could appear under more than one category – this is not a precise classification but a means of helping to identify skills.

Skills can be acquired and then developed at different levels – depending on the nature of the job. A caretaker might well benefit from some skill in relating to other people; a counsellor would need the same skills in much greater depth.

If you're not used to analysing jobs in terms of skills you may need the help of others. Some sample skills lists are given in Appendix B but again these are not meant to be exhaustive.

IDENTIFYING NEEDS

In chapter 2 it was stressed that training shouldn't be programme-centred – taking up a particular package and using it willy-nilly. Instead, the training must be tailored to the particular situation in which the work is being done; specific local needs must be identified.

Local needs can be of two types:

1. People needs – the specific needs of the individuals being trained.

2. Locality needs – needs peculiar to the church or local community.

People needs. These range from the needs of particular individuals to the needs of a whole group being trained.

Ted is sixty, he's never been to a training course before and is apprehensive. Ted's need is to be made to feel secure about doing the job and even in being trained for it. An awareness of Ted's need should affect the design of his training. On the other hand, Mary has done this work before in another church. She has a wealth of experience and skills, and basic training would be wasted on her. Instead, her experience and skill could be tapped in training others.

Training could be designed to allow Mary the opportunity to share from her past. The pastoral team have been confronted by their first case of AIDS. They have no experience of this illness or how to help terminally ill people – this dictates their training agenda at their next monthly meeting.

A whole range of different group and individual needs could be identified. Here are some common ones:

- basic training for those new to the work
- development of new skills for those with some experience
- working at specific problems or issues that have arisen in the work
- helping people to adapt to a changing scene
- renewing of vision – a refresher for those who have been involved for some time
- bringing a team closer together
- working at specific weaknesses and failings
- enabling people to develop in their area of work.

Locality needs include all those things that are unique to the locality and that will influence the content of any training given. A church preparing a team for outreach in the local community might need to take account of the large Muslim and Hindu communities in the area and this might be reflected in the content of any training. The training of Sunday school teachers would have to take into account the three mentally handicapped children who have been integrated into groups.

The 'trainer' must take some responsibility for perceiving these needs through his or her knowledge of the job, the people and the locality. But this is only half the story: those being trained will identify needs of their own – eg their lack of skill, problems they need help with. The trainer must also be prepared to listen to what participants or would-be participants require from the training.

One of the trainer's tasks when designing training activities is to find the appropriate blend between the needs that they perceive and those identified by participants. We will look at this further in chapter 7.

THINGS TO DO

1. Identify any attitudes that need changing in your own church or group before training programmes can be developed.
2. Using the training audit in Appendix A list all the areas of responsibility in your own church or group.
3. Choose one area of the church's life and work and carry out the training audit (Appendix A) Sections 2–5 for those with responsibility in that area.

4
Means of Training

1: Apprenticeship and Supervision

'How did you learn all the ins and outs of this job?' asked the new church member to the church administrator.

'Oh, I was thrown in at the deep end!' came the reply, spoken in such a way as to suggest that this was the best way to learn.

Many who take up responsibilities in the church learn by this means or through its close relation, 'picking it up as you go along'.

Both are ways of learning 'on the job', but both are very inadequate forms of training. They leave the new leader with no preparation and support and give the impression that discovering the hard way is the best way to learn. On-the-job training when used properly can, however, be one of the most effective means of providing initial training to those new to a job. It can also be a means by which the experienced can develop further. It involves using real work as the context in which training occurs. Good on-the-job training does not leave people to sink or swim. Instead it offers some form of guidance and support throughout the training period.

On-the-job training has tremendous advantages

over training courses and conferences. Trainees receive first-hand experience of the activities and the problems that confront a person doing the job. They learn from real life and can rapidly discover what works and what doesn't work. They also learn from seeing more experienced people getting on with the job. The two models described in this chapter – apprenticeship and supervision – have much to commend them as means of training individuals. In the church with few leaders, limited demand for training or where other means of training are impractical, *apprenticeship* or *supervision* schemes come into their own. Both require limited preparation, the minimum of personnel, no special meetings or structures to fit into the church programme, and operate at the convenience of the few (often only two) people involved.

APPRENTICESHIP

Apprenticeship is one of the oldest and most respected ways of training. In chapter 1 we referred to the apprenticeship relationship that existed between Jesus and the disciples and we identified the stages in that training.

In the Church of England the traditional relationship between curate and vicar is that of trainer and apprentice: the curate gradually being given more and more responsibility as he sees the vicar fulfilling his parochial duties. Unfortunately, the value of this training relationship has to some extent been lost. Many curates find themselves left to take responsibility for specific areas of parish life that the vicar has not the time or inclination to be involved with. Instead of observing them at work curates are thrown in at the deep end. Instead of receiving guidance and support they often have to go it alone. Many areas of parish life may be closed to them and they move on with only limited experience.

In essence, apprenticeship involves the person being trained working alongside someone already involved in the work. To begin with they observe and note what is happening. Then they are allowed to take responsibility for parts of the work – being watched over by the experienced worker. When they are ready they take total responsibility, still watched by the experienced worker. And finally they are let loose on their own. Apprenticeship offers immediate experience of the actual work in its real context. It can be arranged at any time without waiting for a course to be set up, and it is flexible – starting and finishing at any time. On the other hand it does depend on the 'trainer' having the ability to provide the right sort of experiences, guidance and support for the apprentice. As a means of training it requires a heavy investment in people, often with a trainer to trainee ratio of one to one, although it is possible for a 'trainer' to take responsibility for a small group. This may be necessary where a number of people require training but only a limited number of experienced leaders are able to take on apprentices. Apprenticeship can be used in a variety of activities in the local church; house group leadership, work with children, youth work, creche helpers, catering team members, worship leaders, events organisers and so on.

Apprenticeship training is spread over a period of time which will be determined by the complexity of the job and the speed with which the person being trained can pick it up. In some of the more complex

roles in the church, such as house group leader or
youth worker, apprenticeship training has the distinct
advantage of allowing the newcomer to ease himself
gradually into the work. As the apprentice gradually
gains in confidence and skill so he, so she, can be given
more responsibility.

SETTING UP APPRENTICESHIP TRAINING

1. Choose someone already involved in leadership
in that area who would make a good 'trainer' (more
details can be found on p. 72 'The work of the trainer'
and in chapter 7). Remember not all Sunday school
teachers or leaders of the catering team are good at
helping other adults to learn. It will often be necessary
to offer the would-be trainer some guidance and
training before they take on responsibility for an
apprentice.

2. Devise a list of the main things that the apprentice
will need to experience and learn in order to do the job.
(It will help if you divide the requirements of the job
into knowledge, attitudes and skills as described in
chapter 3.)

3. Ensure that the apprentice understands the
broader context in which the job or ministry fits, eg the
way house groups fit into the life of the church, the
number and purpose of house groups, the church's
policy on house groups.

4. Encourage the building of open, honest relationships between trainer and apprentice. This won't
necessarily happen automatically. The trainer will
need to help the learner feel relaxed and secure. Many
things can block the development of a good relationship:

– the trainer treating the learner like a child rather than another adult

– the trainer communicating a sense of superiority rather than acting as a servant, open to learning new things himself or herself

– the trainer having little time for the learner and rushing through their meetings.

5. Agree a structure for apprenticeship. This must include a regular time when both can meet to discuss the last work experience.

The needs of the apprentice

1. To understand exactly where their particular job or role fits into the broader work of the church.

2. To know exactly what is expected of them and when – when they will observe, when they will be asked to do something themselves, etc.

3. Tools to help them observe and identify the main learning points from an experience – eg an observation sheet like that illustrated in Case Study 7.

CASE STUDY 7:
Observation sheet used in training people to lead a discussion

1. How did the leader start the discussion?

2. Did this prove helpful to the group? Yes/No
3. Explain why it helped or didn't help the group.

4. The discussion leader will only occasionally take part in the

discussion. After each of his/her contributions decide what each one did for the discussion and tick the relevant statement below:
— added some valuable information
— moved the discussion on
— questioned to help clarify what had been said by others
— encouraged people to get involved
— discouraged following red herrings
— summarized what had been said
— encouraged people
— handled a difficult group member
— encouraged people to express their feelings
— encouraged differences of views to be explored
—
—
—

5. Describe anything the discussion leader *did* that you didn't understand or disagreed with.
6. Note any feelings/emotions observed in group members during the discussion, eg enthusiasm, frustration, anger, surprise, boredom, etc.
7. How do you feel the discussion went?

The work of the trainer

In the days when the old craft trades were taught by apprenticeship, the experienced member of that partnership was called a 'master'. Here we have used the title 'trainer' to describe that role. This may seem a rather specialized title to give to the house group leader who has taken responsibility for helping someone new to the job to learn the ropes. It is important, however, that anyone who takes on such responsibility possesses or acquires some of the knowledge and skills needed to enable the apprentice to learn. The trainer needs to spend time understanding their role before being let loose with an apprentice. This includes:

1. Determining what the apprentice already knows. Has the apprentice any experience of this work from a previous church? Did they do things in the same way? What do they know about the job? What skills or talents do they possess already?

2. Ensuring that the apprentice understands how the job fits into the life and work of the church as a whole. The new mother and toddler group helper needs to understand the reason the church has such a group, whether those who attend belong to the church or have no church interest, the history of the group, etc.

3. Producing, together with the apprentice, a programme of learning that enables the training to proceed in easy stages. Each session can include a special focus on one identified area of skills or procedure. More time can be given to areas of the work where the apprentice lacks any previous knowledge or needs to develop new skills.

4. Demonstrating how the job is done. The trainer becomes a model of good practice but at the same time should be happy to point out when things went wrong or to look at alternative ways of working.

5. Supporting and encouraging the apprentice as he or she starts to take responsibility, a little at a time until he or she is confident enough to take a whole session and then work on their own.

6. Conducting a review that helps the apprentice to think about experiences on the job. During this review the apprentice will be able to share his or her observations and the trainer offer feedback on the way the apprentice handled his or her responsibilities. (See

chapter 7 for more information on giving and receiving feedback.)

Modelling and training

One of the most crucial elements of apprenticeship training is the trainer's ability to model good practice. The trainer who is already involved in the ministry shows the apprentice how to do it. Modelling has the strength of demonstrating quite clearly how things are done. It is a straightforward activity when it involves teaching fairly mechanical or practical skills – playing a game or working a machine, for instance. It is much more difficult in jobs that involve relating to others. There are real dangers with modelling and these must be faced by anyone who uses this method – even the most experienced will model bad practice as well as good. Those who learn from modelling may learn certain things without even realizing it and even with a respected trainer, apprentices can develop unhelpful ways of working. Modelling also has the danger of stifling the special gifts and abilities of the person being trained – the trainer may implant his or her way of doing it and leave little room for another's individuality. In many jobs, especially those involving the use of creative gifts or work with people there is often no *one* right way of behaving – modelling, if misused, can suggest there is!

When modelling is used it must be a deliberate activity. This doesn't mean that the trainer acts artificially in front of the group or in his job but that he is aware that the apprentice is watching the way particular things are done. Both trainer *and* apprentice need to be aware of the dangers. The trainer must be prepared to open his way of doing things to close examination so that the good and the bad can be recognized and explored. The trainer should also provide opportunities to explore alternative ways of handling people or situations – affirming the validity of these alternatives.

Let's see how apprenticeship training may work in practice. Case Study 8 uses youth leadership training as an example.

If when you've read it you feel that this is far from anything you could achieve with people in your church or group then look at Case Study 9 which is provided for those who feel they must start at a less ambitious level.

CASE STUDY 8:
Youth leader apprenticeship training

In this case study we visit a small Baptist church that has opened its doors to the teenagers of the district. The youth club is an open club with one leader who has an assistant. Together they run the club on one evening each week. The club has a regular attendance of 25 teenage boys and girls between the ages of 12 and 16.

Initial meeting

The existing leader, John, and apprentice, Val, met for coffee and a general chat as a means of establishing a relationship. Then John explained the place and purpose of youth work in the church – the aim of the club, a short history, details of the leadership team, some of the tensions with the rest of the church, etc.

Details of the apprenticeship were discussed and agreed:
- clarification of the purpose of the apprenticeship and the roles and expectations of trainer and apprentice.
- provisional date to review the whole apprenticeship after 9 months, with an option to extend the apprenticeship if necessary.

– it was agreed to meet once a week to review the experiences of each club night and to pray together.
– a list of knowledge, attitudes, skills required by a youth leader was drawn up as a means of selecting appropriate focal points for training over the weeks and months. The list included understanding the world of teenagers, building relationships with teenagers, sharing faith through relationships, games and activities suitable for use in clubs, planning programmes, club management, handling behaviour problems, function of leader, leadership style, leading a discussion, etc.
– a book list was given out and one copy of a book on youth work provided for immediate reading.

Personal preparation
Val went away to digest the information about the job and prepare to attend her first club night. Her first objective was to get as involved as possible without taking on any specific responsibility – with the aim of getting to know some of the members and the evening routine. She began to read the book given her.

First club experience
Val attended her first club night, was introduced as someone who was preparing to take on club leadership and was then left to participate in the group programme. She made a mental note of any particular things she wanted to question the youth leader about later.

First review
During the week after the club meeting, Val and John met for $1\frac{1}{2}$ hours to review the first experience. Val was encouraged to share her initial impressions and feelings and to comment on anything that she didn't fully understand. An agreed 'syllabus' was drawn up that allowed her to focus on different elements of the job on particular nights.

Weeks 2 and 3   Leadership styles and function of the leader

Week 4   Programme planning
Week 5   Building relationships with young people
They agreed that although Val was intending to concentrate on specific aspects of the club on specific evenings, there should be a degree of flexibility depending on the situation that actually arose on any evening.

There was some discussion over the two chapters of the book that Val had managed to read during the week and it was agreed to keep the book on the agenda at each review meeting.

The two prayed together before parting.

Second club experience

Val again mixed with club members, building on the friendships begun the week before, participated in activities but also made every attempt to watch the leadership role that John demonstrated: the way he intervened in situations, the points in the programme when he directed, the way he behaved in the less structured parts of the evening.

Second review

The second review focused on leadership as planned, with Val sharing her observations. John then talked about his view of leadership and the roles he felt he wanted to play. Together they looked at the appropriateness of these models and the relative strengths and weaknesses as they had been evident during the evening.

Some leadership principles and practice were drawn out, and left with Val to mull over and to consider how they fitted a biblical picture of servant leadership.

There was no time to discuss the book so this was left over to the next review.

Third club experience

Val focused part of her attention on the way the evening's programme had been put together – remembering the different elements, the proportion of structured to unstructured events, the way informal times were used, etc. The

evening also brought a major behavioural problem as one girl
with an unhappy home background decided to go on the
rampage, disrupting others' activities and destroying prop-
erty.

Third review

At Val's request the review was taken up with the behavioural
problem during the previous club meeting. John began by
encouraging Val to share her own observations, feelings and
comments. John then shared his own feelings and insights.
After exploring the possible causes as well as the effects of the
girl's behaviour, they moved on to discuss discipline and
behaviour in more general terms, focusing on how a leader
handles his or her own feelings as well as dealing with the
situation in the most appropriate ways. The discussion never
narrowed down to just one approved method but allowed for a
variety of possibilities and flexibility of approach. They agreed
that Val should concentrate on programme planning the next
week.

The longer term

The apprenticeship continued over nine months during which
time Val began to take responsibility in the club. At her fifth
club evening, Val was asked to take responsibility for
organizing a games tournament, at the next to work with club
members at the refreshment bar. These experiences were
followed with the chance to lead a discussion and chair a
management meeting. After each of these activities the
emphasis at the review meeting shifted from observation and
comment on John's work and the way the club functioned to
discussion of Val's own involvement and experiences. John
encouraged Val to evaluate her own 'performance' and to
share her feelings (joys, frustrations, fears). It also involved
John in giving Val feedback (see chapter 7) and together
working at alternative ways of working.

These 'practice' sessions enabled Val to identify some of
her strengths and to uncover areas in which she needed to do
some more work.

After nine months it was felt right to bring the apprenticeship to an end with Val taking up her role as a fully-fledged assistant leader. It was made clear that this was not the end to her training which could then continue through other means – conferences, leaders' meetings and supervision (see p. 80).

CASE STUDY 9:
Creche helper apprenticeship training

This study takes place in a large ecumenical church on a housing estate made up mostly of council houses. There are many families with young children. Beryl the new helper in the creche is fifteen. There are three other girls and one boy – all teenagers – who help on a rota basis. Mrs Preston is responsible for the creche. She is good with babies but has no experience in training others. The creche is held during the communion service which starts at ten o'clock every Sunday. There are usually between eight and twelve babies present. The apprenticeship is much less structured than in the previous case study but a minimum amount of guidance and support still takes place.

First creche experience

Beryl was invited to attend the creche after volunteering her services. Mrs Preston invited her to come along and watch what happens. Beryl sits through the creche playing with one or two babies and cuddling one that gets upset. At the end of the session Mrs Preston asks her if she still feels it is what she wants to do. As Beryl seems to have a natural way with babies Mrs Preston accepts her and talks to her about the rota. She also gives Beryl a list of things she will have to look out for during creche. Mrs Preston has produced this with the help of one of the other mums. Mrs Preston explains briefly why they have a creche and what the helpers are meant to do.

Second creche experience
Beryl takes her place as an apprentice. During the session Mrs Preston keeps an eye on Beryl and at the end of the time spends ten minutes talking to her about the way she coped with the situations that arose. This chat, it is agreed, becomes a regular feature of each creche where Beryl is on duty.

The longer term.
Mrs Preston suggests to Beryl that they review the job at the end of a year to see if Beryl wants to continue.

SUPERVISION

Supervision, like apprenticeship, is a form of on-the-job training. It is also ideally suited to the training of individuals and small groups. Unlike apprenticeship it does not involve the trainer in acting as a model or require the trainer's presence at every activity in which the learner is involved. The supervisor's role is more akin to a counsellor than a model – helping people to examine and explore their early experiences on the job and to identify the issues raised, the problems encountered and their own feelings as learners. The supervisor is often more remote from the work situation than the apprenticeship trainer and is able to be more objective when helping the person being trained. The word 'supervisor' conjures up different images to different people. To someone from an industrial background the picture may be that of a short-haired, brown-coated middle manager watching over and checking the quality of the work being done. Someone with experience in the youth service or from a counselling background might see a relaxed listener wearing a baggy jumper, seated in a comfy armchair with a mug of coffee, asking the occasional question and nodding encouragingly. Those from the world of school teaching might remember the well-dressed tutor sitting at the back of a class ready to share observations and give feedback about performance as one professional to another.

In the local church I would suggest that we put the first type of supervision – often called managerial supervision – to one side as it is the least appropriate. Instead we will use a combination of the non-managerial supervision of the youth service and the 'professional' supervision of teacher training. Although supervision is best conducted in an informal atmosphere, it is more than just having a friendly chat.

Choosing a supervisor
The role of a supervisor is a specialist one and the choice should be made with care. Here are some considerations:

1. They should have some knowledge of the work that the person they are supervising is involved in. They may have been actively involved in the past, or be currently involved in similar work in the church or in their work life. For example, a social worker could act as a supervisor to a new church youth leader, someone with a background in education might be able to help a house group leader or Sunday school teacher, a member of the church pastoral team might supervise a new member of that team.

2. They should possess or be encouraged to acquire supervisory skills and be sympathetic with the role of a supervisor. See chapter 7 for more details.

3. They should be able to behave as an 'enabler' rather than a 'superior' checking up on the person being trained. If there is a danger that an elder or

minister might create this impression it is usually better to find someone with a more objective viewpoint.

4. The supervisor could be someone outside the church, from a neighbouring church or from the denominational support services (deanery and diocesan staff in the Church of England, circuit steward in the Methodist Church, etc).

5. The supervisor could be a colleague – another Sunday school teacher or door-to-door visitor.

6. Supervision might on occasions even be a mutual activity – co-supervision where two people in the same or similar ministries supervise each other, each taking time to act as supervisor and supervised.

7. The supervisor must above all be someone with whom the person being supervised can feel relaxed, confident, open and whom he or she respects. It is usually better to let the individual choose his or her own supervisor from inside or outside the church. If this happens the church should make sure that the individuals concerned know what is expected of their supervisory relationship.

Setting up the supervision

In some ways this is similar to preparing apprenticeship training. The supervisor and the person being supervised need to meet to establish their relationship. This should be done quite formally so that it is clear what each expects of the other. A written contract is one way to ensure that both get the best from the relationship. The contract, whether written down formally and signed or just agreed verbally, would contain the following:

- details of how frequently the two will meet and the length of the meetings

- details of the point of the meeting – the topics that will be explored
- an analysis of the job into the skills, knowledge and attitudes that the person being trained will need and the method of assessing progress in these areas
- agreement as to the total length of the supervisory contract – a year, two years or whatever
- agreement about when and how frequently the supervisor will observe the trainee at work.

The supervisory meeting

A major feature of this form of training is the meeting between supervisor and learner. The frequency of this will depend on those involved and should be mutually agreed between them. They may find it helpful to meet more frequently in the early days, reducing the frequency as the trainee becomes more established in his or her role. Meetings should include the following:

1. *Listening* – a time for the person being trained to openly share thoughts, feelings and tensions. The supervisor listens while the person involved in pastoral counselling shares what happened at her last visit to the house of the bereaved husband, the hospital visitor talks about the last visit, the new Boys' Brigade officer talks about their last evening programme. The supervisor listens, trying to help the learner identify the way the experience affected him or her. Together they examine other relevant influences – spiritual needs and problems, pressures on the family, anxiety caused by the expectations of others, etc.

2. *Examining* the particular skills, knowledge and attitudes that supervisor and learner have agreed are essential requirements for the job. At each meeting they will focus on any that have been practised or developed during the trainee's last involvement in

their particular area of ministry. It may be useful, to
devise a schedule (similar to the one described in the
section headed 'Apprenticeship', p. 68) that encourages the person being trained to focus on particular
skills or areas of knowledge on particular occasions.
This is more appropriate to some activities than
others. For instance it would be inappropriate to ask
someone being supervised in counselling to focus on
confrontation skills in their next counselling session.
On the other hand it would be reasonable to ask a
playgroup worker to try out their storytelling skills at
their next playgroup.

3. *Problem-solving* – focusing on specific issues and
problems which arose during the trainee's last work
experience. The supervisor uses his or her skill to
encourage the trainee to explore solutions rather than
simply offering potted advice. In this way the new
leader can learn to solve problems rather than relying
on others.

4. *Offering feedback*. When the supervisor has
observed the trainee in action they will want to offer
feedback. The supervisor and trainee should decide
the time and frequency of any observation visits. It is
valuable to have these visits coincide with occasions
when the person under training is trying out
particular skills. Again this precise focus of attention
will only be appropriate in certain types of work.
Offering feedback requires care and a level of skill (see
chapter 7).

5. *Prayer/encouragement*. Encouragement is a vital
role of the supervisor. This includes affirming the
trainee's strengths, acknowledging his or her progress, and giving support as the trainee tries to resolve
any problems. Ways of encouraging may also include
opportunities to focus on the learner's spiritual

growth and development and a regular reminder of reliance on God through times of prayer.

It is clear that supervisory training leaves trainees less supported when they are on the job than apprenticeship. Those being supervised need some knowledge or training before they start work and it may be helpful if they have done some reading or attended a course before they are let loose. As the supervisor doesn't stand over them while they are taking the house group or Sunday school class, they will need someone (other than their supervisor) to be on hand in case a problem arises. This might be an experienced house group leader who sits in or works alongside the trainee (but not in an apprenticeship relationship) or it could be the Sunday school leader working with the neighbouring group.

Supervision as a means of training lends itself to a variety of ministries in the church but has a special part to play in ministries where building relationships is central to the work (eg counselling, visiting). Supervisory training is most effective when linked with other forms of training such as distance learning (see chapter 5), or attendance at training courses (see chapter 6).

CASE STUDY 10:
Supervision of a pastoral counsellor

Shirley is a member of a growing Anglican church situated in a small market town. She has been invited by her church to join a small group who share the work of pastoral counselling. Her natural ability to get alongside others and her nursing background have been important considerations for those making the decision. Because of the specialist nature of this work she agreed to attend a course in counselling at the local technical college. This ran over ten evenings. She was urged at this course to continue 'training' by finding a supervisor who could help her reflect on experiences she encountered when counselling people. Shirley has asked another member of the church pastoral team, Pat, to act as her supervisor.

Initial supervisory meeting

Shirley and Pat spent an evening talking over the nature of the supervision, both sharing their expectations of such a relationship. Pat felt that she could cope with the role described. They agreed that they would meet after any counselling Shirley was asked to undertake, to reflect on the experience. They agreed to review their relationship after six months.

First counselling session

Shirley was asked to visit an elderly woman who had recently been bereaved. With her husband, she had been an occasional visitor at the church. The widow was distraught, her husband's death being sudden and without warning. They had been very close, their only child now living overseas. Shirley listened most of the evening, hearing a mixture of sorrow and guilt and memories. She agreed to return, believing that the widow needed help and support in coping with the early stages of bereavement, but not sure at this stage in what way to help.

First supervisory review

Two days later, as soon as they could arrange to meet, Pat and Shirley reviewed the experience. Pat allowed Shirley time to describe what had happened, what she had said and observed, how she had felt during the session and the questions she came away with. Pat asked probing questions in an attempt to understand more clearly herself, and as a means of helping Shirley to think more deeply. They thought together about the next step and how much initiative Shirley should take at the next meeting. They also discussed confidentiality and how much of the details of the counselling sessions Shirley should share with Pat.

Second supervisory review
This took place eight days later, after Shirley's second visit to the widow. Shirley had found this a more distressing time as emotions had been high, sorrow mingled with anger. Shirley found some of the anger hard to handle, saying things she wasn't sure were particularly helpful. This became the focus of the supervision. Pat allowed Shirley time to express her own feelings during and after the visit. They explored a variety of alternative ways of handling anger.

The longer term
The supervision continued, Pat doing very little directing but trying to be positive in helping Shirley to sort out what was happening and to think about the way ahead during the visits. The supervisory relationship continued through two other counselling situations in which Shirley was involved. It was inappropriate for Pat to sit in on any of Shirley's counselling sessions so she was not able to give feedback from her direct observations although she was able to feed back to Shirley what she perceived during their times together.

Continuing care and support
Supervision is often seen as a training support activity during a person's early experiences in a new job or with new responsibility. Some roles in the church require ongoing support that could be supplied through supervision. This is especially true of those who work with others – ministers, elders, house group leaders, pastors, youth workers and children's workers. Working with other people can be particularly draining and those with heavy responsibilities in these areas of church life may benefit from long-term supervision.

Contracts need to be worked out detailing the frequency of meetings and the expectations that each side bring to these meetings. The time when the supervisor and worker meet would be taken up with sharing of issues, pressures, problems, feelings related to the work. The supervisor will want to help the worker identify how his or her role is affecting other areas of his or her life; it is important, in monitoring involvement, to see the whole picture. Continuing training needs may also be examined and addressed. Prayer and encouragement continue to remain part of the agenda for each meeting.

Supervision can also be used as a temporary means of training support at any stage of a person's ministry. Someone who has been heavily involved in evangelism for a number of years might decide to attend a conference or course as a means of renewing their vision and seeking new ideas or approaches. Supervisory support for the duration of, or immediately after, the conference can be a valid way of helping the evangelist integrate any new learning into his or her ministry. This relationship may be as short-lived as two or three meetings.

In some cases one-to-one support is replaced by group support and supervision. A team of house group leaders, children's workers or counsellors could support each other through their regular team meetings. Time would have to be given to allow each member of the team to share their experiences or concerns with the rest of the team, who would then take the support/supervisory role. One of the functions of such a group would be to identify future training needs and when similar training needs surface in a number of members, training can then be designed for the group as a whole.

THINGS TO DO

1. Identify people in your church who could act as:
   a) apprenticeship trainers   b) supervisors
   Look for those who already have the experience that is necessary or who have personalities that lend themselves to these forms of supportive training.
2. Take one ministry or job carried out in your church by 'non-professionals' and plan how an apprenticeship or supervisory scheme could be used to train a new leader. Use the three case studies to help you in your planning but adapt them to fit the people, skills and needs of your own situation. Even if you cannot carry the scheme out the planning may be of value at some later date.

5
Means of Training
2: Distance Training

St Edwalds is a parish church in the middle of rural East Anglia. It has a regular congregation of twenty, a choir of five and a children's church consisting of eight children with ages between five and fourteen. It also has the privilege of having one tenth of a minister (the local vicar has nine other village churches in his care). There are a limited number of activities centred around the church. There is no one at St Edwalds with training skills or experience. What happens, therefore, when a member of this small rural church decides they would like some training – as a Sunday school teacher, or church warden, or chairperson of a committee?

There are numerous situations when a *trainer* may not be on hand to offer training. Like St Edwalds, the church may be very small and isolated. It may lack leadership (professional or volunteers). The training needs may be limited to one person or to a very specialist area. The demand for training may arise at a time when other means of training, such as a course or conference, cannot be used.

Distance training is training without the trainer. It's a form of do-it-yourself training that relies heavily on the use of books, correspondence courses, video programmes and the like. It places the burden of responsibility for learning on to the learner in a way that other training doesn't, but it has advantages too.

Advantages

1. Offers the possibility of training for the individual (or group) who wants to be trained but has no one to offer training help.
2. Provides training for those with specialist needs that cannot be catered for in other ways.
3. Can be carried out in a person's own home.
4. Can be carried out at any time and at the pace of the individual or group concerned.
5. Is one form of training that can be undertaken as needs arise in the trainee's own experience.
6. Very economical, especially if the materials (books etc.) are re-usable.

Disadvantages

1. A difficult way of learning for those who are not used to the self-discipline or who find reading difficult.
2. The stimulus of interaction with others being trained may be lost.
3. There is often no one to help and support the learner – to explain things they do not understand.
4. It is often theoretical rather than practical in emphasis.
5. The trainee may have no way of gauging how they are doing.
6. Transferring knowledge/skills/ attitudes from studies to real situations is sometimes difficult for those who use this method.

Distance training can be initiated and controlled by an individual or group looking for new ideas, solutions or skills to meet a need that has arisen in their work in the local church. When Jim, who has recently agreed to take over the care of the shrubs in the graveyard, goes into his local bookshop for a useful book on the subject he is prepared to be 'trained at a distance'.

It is also possible for other leaders in the church to initiate and encourage some form of distance learning. Jim may be *given* the book on shrubs and encouraged to read it. In some churches distance training may be seen as one component in its continuing training programmes.

There are distinct advantages of encouraging those learning through distance training to work in pairs or even small groups. This can be particularly helpful to people who have not undertaken formal learning for a long time or whose experience of formal education has been painful. Those who have never been able to master the self-discipline of working through a book or project also benefit from the support of a close-knit group working together.

CHOOSING MATERIAL: A GUIDE

Material to be used for distance training must be selected to fit in with the needs of those being trained.

Basic training. Where the trainee has little or no experience of the task they are being called to do, distance materials should be used as a way of *supplementing* on-the-job or course-based training. A textbook covering basic information, or a do-it-yourself pack to help a group, could be used. But as a sole means of offering basic training these are second best – only to be used if other means of training are out of the question.

Problem-solving. Those who are already involved in a particular ministry may need to work at a problem that has arisen and for which they need some guidance. A person involved in counselling is confronted with the distraught parents of a glue sniffer for the first time and feels the need to discover more information about it before they meet together again.

Supplementary training. Those involved in apprenticeship training or a particular training course may benefit from distance training to provide more depth or to allow more to be covered. A course for youth workers on using simulation games might require them to read background material before or after a practical session during which a variety of games are tried out.

Updating. Experienced leaders may need to update and refresh their thinking and leadership. An experienced church administrator takes charge of a new computer and uses the manual as a training tool to develop the necessary skills to use it. The worship group agrees to read and discuss the latest book on worship in the church.

TYPES OF DISTANCE TRAINING MATERIALS

1. *Books*. Books tackling a variety of issues – from emotional problems (of interest to those in pastoral counselling) to ways of integrating teenagers into the church (for youth leaders) – are published by the cart-load. It's worth looking through the specialist books in big university bookshops which may not be

written with the church in mind but often contain extremely helpful material. Of particular help are those books that encourage readers to respond in some way to information or ideas contained in the chapters. This is often done through the use of questions or 'things to do' at the end of each chapter. This extra help is important because many who try to learn in this way need help to transfer the words on the page into their own experience.

2. *Videos*. A small number of videos have been produced by Christian organizations as distance learning tools. Usually these are put together in such a way as to help those being trained to reflect on and relate the video programme to their own situations. Video training programmes designed for use in Christian groups already exist on topics like evangelism, house group leadership and Sunday school teaching. Some of these programmes rely on group work and are inappropriate for individuals who want to learn on their own. These packages usually contain a leader's guide with detailed instructions on how to run the programme, and material for participants which may be in the form of handouts to read or a workbook to fill in.

There are many more Christian videos that the producers classify as training videos but which are, in effect, recordings of people giving talks or preaching sermons. These only really become training tools (if we accept the definition of training offered in this book) when used as *part* of the training programme or as a means of supplementing practical work of some kind. This is one example of the confusion that exists over the use and meaning of the word 'training'. Many so-called training videos are really general teaching programmes and are not designed to help people develop practical abilities for a specific job or ministry.

High quality video training programmes have been pioneered by those involved in management and business training, and some of the programmes available from organizations such as Video Arts or Gower TFI (see resources guide in chapter 8) can be used in the context of the local church. The major drawback is the high cost of hiring.

Video is a convenient and exciting medium to use. It can bring real or simulated incidents to life in someone's sitting room, where they can be viewed and reviewed, discussed and dissected at leisure.

Any church with the money and a small amount of expertise could produce its own video distance training material. In the Sunday school a recording could be made of a teacher telling a story to the 5–7s age group. A house group discussion could be recorded. The church council meeting could be filmed to help future chairpeople explore the skills of chairing. To produce a library of short videos would require a home video camera, sufficient lighting, and a knowledge of what to look at and focus on in the filming. It would also be helpful to produce a set of guidelines to help users of the video to observe and reflect on what made for good and bad practice on the part of those who were recorded. The end product will not be a professional training programme but a tool that could be used as part of someone's training for particular work.

3. *Correspondence courses*. These are training courses produced by a training agency, which offer step-by-step guidance through the material, and a link with a 'tutor' who will receive, mark and return written projects. The course may be in the form of a booklet

containing 'lectures' in written form followed by questions to answer and possibly essays to write. Structure and support are built into the programme through the use of step-by-step instructions and the link with a tutor. These can be advantages for lone learners unused to working on their own. Some courses involve meeting the tutor on one or more occasions to talk about progress and to work at difficult parts of the course. Correspondence courses may be chiefly theoretical, designed to pass on knowledge and understanding or may include practical and project work to encourage the trainee to put skills and knowledge into practice.

A number of theological and Bible colleges offer correspondence courses but only a few of these are designed to train people in a practical way for ministry.

A church might consider devising its own correspondence course. This could be useful if there is a regular and heavy demand for training and where some expertise in writing and tutoring exists.

4. *Television.* Some programmes are designed for training, like those shown through the Open University or the Open Tech. Don't write these off as being too academic and theoretical for church use. Some are very practical and may not be designed for full-time degree courses. Popular television programmes may also offer useful background material for training, by focusing on issues important for those working with children and teenagers, for example, or for the evangelism team or those involved in counselling. These are not distance training programmes and would need to be used in conjunction with group discussion or practical work to ensure their practical value.

5. *Computers.* Education programmes that help people develop skills of decision-making and problem-solving abound and can be found for most makes of popular computers – BBC, Amstrad, Commodore, IBM. There are also computer programmes on using a computer. Many of the computer packages use a method of training called programmed learning. The computer asks questions or poses problems that the trainee answers, and the computer then moves on to the next stage depending on the answer. In this way incorrect responses can be corrected or a variety of alternative solutions can be explored. The computer acts as the trainer – moving people on at their own pace depending on their grasp of what has gone before.

6. *Interactive video.* A more recent development of computer-based programmed learning has involved linking videos and computer to produce a learning tool used in industry and called interactive video. The video presents situations that the trainee responds to by feeding in decisions on the computer. The computer then searches the video for a further situation to illustrate the consequences of the trainee's decision. This imaginative combination is limited in its use to those with the necessary equipment but one day it may well be available for use in the local church.

7. *Slides/soundstrips/films/cassettes.* These are all similar to video in their use as distance training tools. They suffer one big disadvantage over video in that they are not as flexible or convenient to use.

In utilizing distance training the local church needs:

    1. to know what is available
    2. to know how to obtain it
    3. to have sufficient finances

We will look at items 1 and 2 in more detail in chapter 8.

GETTING THE MOST OUT OF DISTANCE TRAINING

Distance training as a means of developing individuals or groups in their ministry puts most of the responsibility for learning onto the trainee. This may be too much for some to cope with. Distance training may not be very effective when used on its own and is best used in conjunction with some form of supervision.

Here are six steps to improve the effectiveness of distance training:

1. Identify the training needs of those involved by discussion with them – ie, basic, supplementary, updating, specific problem.

2. Find the appropriate training material. This may involve being highly selective – chapter of a book rather than the whole book, section of a video or a correspondence course.

3. If possible clarify with the trainee the focus of their training. List specific items they are looking at or for, and what they want to do as a result of what they learn, ie how it should affect their work.

4. Structure the training if it involves a lot of work or if the person being trained would benefit from such guidelines. Set targets and projects so that they know what to do and when.

5. After each major section of their work help them reflect on what they have done. Spend time with them allowing them to talk about their reading/viewing etc and to share its impact on them. Give them time to ask about things they haven't understood.

6. Help them to transfer what they have learned to their actual work. This can be done through reflection – the trainee can be encouraged to think about what she will do back in the old people's group or women's fellowship as a result of her training. It can also be encouraged by setting particular projects that help them put new insights into practice. The women's group leader who has been reading about shared leadership might be encouraged to work out a plan for sharing the leadership with others in her group.

CASE STUDY 11:
Distance training in evangelism – use of a commercial package

Three churches on the edge of a city have got together for outreach into the local community. They have agreed on a project in which small discussion groups will be set up in people's homes and used to attract interested friends. The churches have agreed to explore the use of an evangelism training package produced by a Christian agency.

A small group made of representatives from each church have met to examine a course sampler provided on video by the producers.

This training package includes video programmes, a detailed leader's guide and workbooks for each participant.

Initial planning

After viewing the sampler it was agreed to hire the package for three months and to use the early parts for all those involved in the prospective home groups and the more specialist parts of the programme with those who would be leading.

Two church leaders agreed to share in the leadership of the actual course. Dates were agreed.

Pre-course planning
Invitations were sent out, and the training pack was hired. The two course leaders previewed the course material and decided how to use it to meet their particular needs. The leaders had no formal training as trainers or as speakers but they were recognized as being able to communicate with others and to organize the course material. The leader's guide provided all the instruction they needed to conduct the course.

Conducting the course
The course consisted of six evenings of fairly intensive work spread over six weeks. The sessions included watching a video programme, followed by work in small groups, based on instructions given in a workbook. After each evening there was homework for individuals to get on with until the next meeting. The course leaders tried to monitor how all those attending were coping with the course. That gave extra support to individuals who seemed to run into difficulties during the training.

The seventh and eighth weeks consisted of preparation for the small groups and on the ninth week the discussion groups began.

Three months later
The original members of the training course met to evaluate the whole project. They looked at how valuable the training package had been as a way of preparing people for their discussion groups, and the effectiveness of the groups themselves. As a result of the evaluation, various suggestions were made for improving any future training.

This training package is an example of a highly structured distance training programme, designed for groups, with a practical emphasis and requiring minimum training skills on the part of those organizing it.

THINGS TO DO

1. Discover if any distance training materials already exist in your church, eg books on Sunday school teaching, a manual for sidesmen, filmstrips on leading a small group. Make a list and look for ways of making them available for anyone who might need them.
2. Examine any distance training courses already being used by individuals and groups in your church. Discover how they are used and, in the light of information in this chapter, explore whether they could be used more effectively.

6
Means of Training

3: Planning and Running Training Courses

In chapter 4 we looked at **apprenticeship and supervision,** which were described as *on-the-job* training. In this chapter we consider the use of training **courses and conferences,** which can also be referred to as *off-the-job* training – in other words, training that takes place away from the real work situation.

Courses can be completely home-made, organized and staffed by the local church and run in the church hall, or even in someone's home. Alternatively, they may be locally organized but staffed by trainers from outside the local church. A third option is that a course is organized and run by agencies outside the local church altogether.

Training courses are not necessarily an alternative to the other means of training already described but may be used to supplement on-the-job training. They may also be used as one element in a church's continuing training programme.

Off-the-job training also has its advantages and disadvantages.

Advantages	*Disadvantages*
1. A useful means of training a *group* of leaders at the same time.	1. Those involved in organizing and running such events require the necessary skills.
2. Allows those involved in similar work or at similar stages to support one another through the training they are undergoing.	2. It may be difficult to find a convenient time when all interested parties are available to attend.
3. Can free people to experiment with new ideas/behaviour/skills in an atmosphere where there is little at stake if they get it wrong.	3. May have an artificial feel about it because it is away from the 'real work'.
4. An ideal way to help people practise difficult skills with no risk to others, eg counselling skills.	4. Participants often need help in transferring what they have learned to their job or role.
5. Ideal for focusing on specific issues that might not arise conveniently during on-the-job training.	5. Sometimes unable to meet all the individual needs and expectations that participants bring with them to a course.
6. An opportunity to step back from the 'real work', to reflect on and evaluate past experiences, and to think more objectively about applying new learning to the real work.	6. Courses may create unrealistic expectations in participants and cause feelings of frustration or inadequacy.
	7. Can add extra time pressures to busy people.

Advantages	*Disadvantages*
7. More skills and understanding can be concentrated into a relatively short period of time.	8. There is often a shortage of good courses.

Training courses are distinct events – they may last a few hours during a day or evening, or may consist of a series of days or evenings. They are distinct from *training programmes* which refer to a church's continuing strategy for training, spread over years. See chapter 3 for more information on training programmes.

INTERNAL OR EXTERNAL?

An important decision to make when planning training courses is whether to run the course internally or to use courses organized by outside agencies. Both have merits and weaknesses, and a combination may be desirable.

INTERNAL COURSES
planned and run by the local church

Advantages	*Disadvantages*
1. Can be planned to meet the training needs in your group.	1. If there is a rapid turnover of leadership the demand for courses may be more than the church can cope with, especially if they are relying
2. Can be run at a time that will best suit members of your group.	
3. Those who attend will work with	

Advantages

people they already
know and with whom
they feel secure. This
may speed up the
process of learning.

4. There is continuing
support from the other
course participants
after it's over.

5. A way of recognizing
and using the gifts/
skills/experiences of
people in the church.

6. Learning is more
easily transferred to
the real world. Any
problems in putting
the course material
into practice can be
worked at with
those who carried
out the training.

7. The pace of the
training can be
modified to match
the pace of the group;
there is no need to
cram everything in
at one time.

8. Costs can be kept to
a minimum (the cost
of people's time is,
conveniently, a
hidden cost).

Disadvantages

totally on courses
which are organized
internally.

2. Those designing and
running courses
need some trainer
skills.

3. Some adults may
feel embarrassed to
be trained with
others in their
church, knowing
that they will have
to live with any
'mistakes' or
'embarrassments'
that occur during the
course.

4. Some course
members may be
reluctant to accept
an internal trainer
and demand an
'expert' from
outside.

5. Course content may
be narrow and
lacking in originality,
reinforcing old ideas
and methods rather
than encouraging
the new.

EXTERNAL COURSES
Organized and run by agencies outside the local church

Advantages

1. Specialist trainer expertise usually available.
2. Some participants may be more willing to take risks in learning and practising new things if they are with people they don't know so well.
3. Ideal if there aren't enough in one church requiring training.
4. Ideal if church hasn't time to run a course.
5. Mixing with people from different backgrounds and experience produces a greater wealth of ideas and resources.

Disadvantages

1. Training may not meet the exact needs of the local church.
2. The church has no control over the timing of courses, which may be held at inconvenient times.
3. Some adults may feel very insecure because of the unfamiliar environment in which the training takes place.
4. Many adults have problems in transferring what they learned on the course to the work in their local church.

The rest of this chapter is aimed at those who wish to set up and run their own, home-grown training courses. More information on external courses can be found in chapter 8.

DESIGNING A TRAINING COURSE: A STEP-BY-STEP GUIDE TO COURSE DESIGN

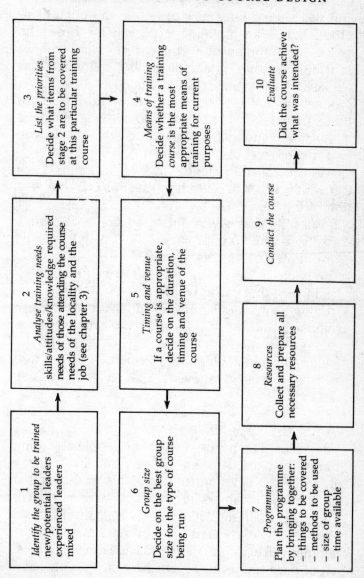

1
Identify the group to be trained
new/potential leaders
experienced leaders
mixed

2
Analyse training needs
skills/attitudes/knowledge required
needs of those attending the course
needs of the locality and the
job (see chapter 3)

3
List the priorities
Decide what items from
stage 2 are to be covered
at this particular training
course

4
Means of training
Decide whether a training
course is the most
appropriate means of
training for current
purposes

5
Timing and venue
If a course is appropriate,
decide on the duration,
timing and venue of the
course

6
Group size
Decide on the best group
size for the type of course
being run

7
Programme
Plan the programme
by bringing together:
 – things to be covered
 – methods to be used
 – size of group
 – time available

8
Resources
Collect and prepare all
necessary resources

9
Conduct the course

10
Evaluate
Did the course achieve
what was intended?

Steps 1–2: The initial groundwork
Details of steps 1 and 2 have been covered in chapter 3 and you should refer back to ensure thorough planning. There is a temptation, especially for those who are used to organizing courses, to plan without consulting those undergoing the training. This obviously saves time, but it can also be counter-productive: it lowers the motivation and interest of those invited. Where participants have been involved in the design and timing of the course there is likely to be a higher level of commitment.

You can consult potential trainees in a number of different ways. You could try using one or a combination of the following:
– a questionnaire given out to all potential participants, asking for information about people's needs and timing of courses.
– interviews or, if you prefer, informal chats, with a sample of those who would attend the course.
– setting up a joint planning group made up of those who will staff the courses and representatives from the participants.
– setting up a joint planning group made up of those who will staff the event and all who will be attending.

Step 3: List the priorities
'Indigestion' is a major ailment for people attending training courses. It often comes from the trainer's concern to cover as much as possible in the limited time available. Trainers often act as if there may never be another training event, so that all the essential items must be covered. An evening or a day is crammed full of information on a wide range of topics. Course participants may even share the illusion that if

their notebooks aren't full at the end of the course their time hasn't been well spent.

The fact is that all adults have a limited capacity for learning new things, and for many adults this capacity is severely restricted. Participants may leave a course with a full notebook but with very little chance of transferring the information into practice. Those many adults that cannot take notes are likely to go away confused or numb!

If training is to have a strong practical emphasis there must be time for people to get involved, to try things out and to practise certain skills. Practical methods cut down the amount of information that can be handled at a course. These limitations need to be recognized and accepted when deciding what to include in a course and what to leave to another time.

When it comes to selecting the topics to be included, take the following into consideration:

1. *The experience of the people involved.* A course for new leaders will major on those areas of skill, knowledge and attitudes that are essential to start out on the job. Those new to chairing committees will need some early help in how to formulate an agenda. The new Sunday school teacher will need help on how to put a lesson together. Even by prioritizing in this way there may be important items that have to be left to another occasion.

2. *The pressing needs.* If training courses are being organized for those already involved in the work, then their pressing needs may help you to identify what to include on the course. For example, 'making worship more lively' may be the major theme at a course for the worship group that has got into a rut; 'handling difficult questions' may be tackled with door-to-door

visitors who have recently been confronted with questions they couldn't answer.

Sometimes it may only be possible to tackle one topic at a training event. An evening for the drama group could focus solely on 'projecting the voice' – allowing time to look at principles, and an opportunity for everyone to have a go and to receive some feedback.

Step 4: Deciding to run a course

After going through the first three steps it is worth-while to stop and ask the question, 'Is a training course the best means of meeting the needs we have identified?' It may be that the people asking for training are so few and their needs so specialized that some form of supervised reading, or an external course, would be most appropriate. If the trainees are all new to the work, apprenticeship or supervision may be more appropriate, especially if potential supervisors or apprenticeship trainers are available.

A training course will be particularly appropriate if:
 i) a number of people want to undergo training in the same topics, especially if teams are involved.
 ii) the numbers involved are too many for a super-visory or apprenticeship training.
iii) the topics to be covered include skills that can best be practised away from the home situation.
 iv) the course is used to complement other means of training.
 v) the training involves a group wanting to work at a specific problem or need together.

Refer back to chapters 4 and 5 to help you make your decision.

Step 5: Duration, timing and venue

Is the course to last a day or an evening? Is it part of a

series? Again, consultation with those involved is vital if you want to get it right. Certain evenings of the week may be more suitable than others for some people. Saturdays may be out unless they are mentioned to people six months ahead. Training sessions may be best fitted into the existing leaders' meetings, to avoid adding to the burden of those who live very busy lives.

The venue for training also needs to be carefully considered. It may be convenient to use the church premises or someone's home if the facilities are adequate or if travelling time needs to be kept to a minimum. On the other hand going away to a conference centre or using an 'out-of-town' venue for the day can remove unnecessary distractions and temptations that come with familiar surroundings. Going away also makes the event a little more special, but will add to the cost of holding it.

Step 6: Group size
The size of the group attending a training event has more effect on the training than many realize. Training a group of 300 produces different problems from training a group of one. The more people, the more complex the training process. The main reason for this is that each person who attends is unique and brings their own special needs as well as their very special personalities, their unique past experiences, their own style of learning.

Mrs Jones is sixty, she has been flower arranging for forty years, has a stubborn independent streak, and learns best when she sees things demonstrated by someone else. Mrs Peters is fifty, has just taken up flower arranging, is open and eager to learn and needs to have a go herself before she feels happy. Mrs Jones and Mrs Peters may both be attending the same course on 'Flower arranging for festivals' but each may react in a completely different way to the course. Multiply these differences by six or ten for a course involving a small group and by 300 for a large group. The larger the course the more chance there is that individual needs will not be met.

If training is to meet the needs of those who attend and lead people into more effective ways of working for God, then the smaller the group the better. One-to-one training and training with small groups are the ideal. But there are occasions when a large number of people require training and when it is not possible to run a course more than once.

Before planning a training programme in detail, think about the numbers attending. Even if the numbers are small be prepared to work in different groupings at different times on the course. Your choice of groupings will, to a large extent, be governed by what you want to do and will need to be linked with the subjects being considered and the methods used.

Where there is only one trainer on a course it may be tempting to keep people together as one group for the whole time. This is only necessary where the trainer wants tight control over the whole group. This control may be necessary where the trainer has important information that everyone needs, such as instructions for an exercise or project. Hopefully the trainer will not feel the need to have such control over the whole direction of the course. (To pursue this topic refer to chapter 7: The role and function of the trainer.)

It is possible for one trainer to guide the activities of a great many pairs, trios or small groups within one room, as long as he or she is happy to give groups freedom to get on with their tasks.

Here is a guide to the usefulness of different group sizes:

1. Individual work is useful on a course when you want people to think carefully about themselves or their own experiences, and can offer people the space and quiet in which to think. Exercises involving personal awareness may start off with individual reflection. Questionnaires may be tackled initially by individuals. Practical work may require people to try things out on their own. Some people need the space and the quiet that a short period of personal reflection or activity allows.

2. Pairs are a useful, versatile grouping. They provide a way of helping those who are shy or embarrassed to participate in discussion (sharing in pairs before sharing in the larger group). They provide initial support for learning during an exercise. They are ideal for role play exercises, and some counselling training. They can help people to recognize the value of other people's experience and to begin to see beyond their own limited horizons.

3. Threes are a useful extension of pairs and provide an observer for a pairs exercise. They have a similar function to pairs – providing support for those who are not used to training and learning.

4. Small groups of 4–8 are valuable as work groups or problem-solving groups, where a variety of experiences/skills/knowledge can be brought to bear on a project or a problem. They are good for training those who have to work in small groups – house group leaders, outreach team, Bible study group. They are the unit for training people in being sensitive to group process and group dynamics. They are one of the most commonly used groups at training events.

5. The medium group of 9–30 (this may be the whole

course) is useful for communicating factual information quickly. It is a means of preserving a feeling of one-ness when smaller groupings are used at times during the course: the whole course meets for report-back sessions to receive smaller groups' findings in terms of discussion, projects, solutions etc. This group is too large to be the only unit at a training course as it cuts down the opportunity for involvement, reflection, sharing, practising skills, etc.

6. The large group (30+) may be rarely or never used in a local church context. It has severe limitations as a training group because of the complexity caused by size. Hopefully large numbers like this attending a course will be divided into smaller groupings (see above) for various activities, coming together only for certain whole course activities such as the general course introduction, short talks or lectures, worship, selective sharing of what has been learned.

Step 7: Planning the programme
Course planning involves matching the content of the course (ie the topics to be covered) with suitable methods and groupings of participants, and planning these into the time available. Again it's important not to give in to the temptation to fill every available minute with the 'course content'. Time must also be allowed for:
1. Creating a suitable atmosphere for learning.
2. Worship and devotional times.
3. Helping participants begin to apply their course learning to their real situations.

These will be considered more fully under Step 9 below.

CHOOSING METHODS

Time and care should be taken over the selection of appropriate training methods. Methods are not, as some people view them, just gimmicky ways of passing on information. They are ways of structuring the learning so that people get the most out of the experience and can act as a result of it. A great deal has already been written about methods for helping adults learn in *Making Adult Disciples* and what is written here is complementary to much of that. A trainer is someone who is able to employ a variety of learning methods, selecting the appropriate method for the task in hand. Here are some principles to consider when choosing methods:

1. Training is essentially a practical activity calling for methods that involve participants in trying out skills, applying information or practising new behaviour. Workshops, practicals and experiential learning exercises are amongst those methods that encourage this.

2. Adults have their own experiences to draw from and can learn much from sharing their experiences with each other on a course. Methods that allow for sharing of experiences can be a valuable means of training, eg open discussion, buzz groups. Structuring this kind of sharing can prevent it from becoming an exercise in 'sharing ignorance'.

3. Many adults see training courses as times when they take on the role of learner. Their experiences of learning in the past and their expectations of the trainer often create obstacles to real learning. They may feel insecure, embarrassed, anxious. They may expect lectures and note-taking and be reluctant to

participate in activities. They may want to be told answers and be unwilling to discover for themselves. Some methods need to be used that will help them to feel secure, eg icebreakers, short illustrated talks, pairs and small group exercises.

4. Adults have problems in transferring what they have learned at a course back to their real work. Methods need to be used during the course that can help them to do this – methods that encourage them to keep referring skills/information/ideas/principles back to *their* group or *their* job. Reflection exercises are useful in achieving this, with questions such as: 'How will you use this when you get back?'

5. Many adults find it difficult to grasp vague, abstract ideas. Methods that encourage people to think about concrete examples with real people and situations are always useful, eg case studies, role play.

6. Adults learn more effectively when they are involved. Methods that keep talks and lectures to a minimum and increase involvement through discussion or activity should be used, eg fish bowls, games, workshops, problem-solving exercises.

7. Certain types of training are more appropriate to particular methods, eg principles and ideas can be readily communicated through talks and discussions; skills training requires practical methods like workshops and practicals; sensitivity and awareness training, or the developing and changing of attitudes, all require human relations exercises that encourage people to think about themselves.

8. Different adults have different preferences for the way they learn. Some enjoy talks and can concentrate for long periods of time, others like to get involved, some take in more by observing, others through trying things out. At a well designed training course a variety

of methods will be employed in an attempt to cater for the different preferences.

9. Training should be a good experience where adults can actually discover the fun of learning, eg through learning games and activities with an element of humour.

Below is a summary of a number of training/learning methods with examples of their use. The ideal group size is given as a guide, the time required to conduct one exercise using this method is given as a range. Again this is only a rough guide. Some of these methods are explained in more detail below the diagram, others will have to be followed up in other literature.

Method	Group size	Description	Example	Time required
Agenda formulation	Any size	Invite those attending a course to list their training needs as a means of deciding what to put into the course. Can be carried out as the first exercise during the course or prior to the course beginning.	Half-day refresher course for sidesmen. Spend ten minutes asking the group to work in pairs deciding their most urgent training needs. List on OHP and prioritize.	10–20 mins
Brainstorm	Any size	A means of collecting a wide range of ideas or solutions to a topic or problem. The rules are that participants call out any thought – however wild or remote. Every item is listed without discussion. Discussion follows when ideas are exhausted.	How do we solve the problem of failing to welcome all newcomers to the church on Sunday?	10–30 mins

Method	*Group size*	*Description*	*Example*	*Time required*
Closed circuit television	Small group	Using a video camera, video recorder and TV set, film people practising a skill, or involved in a real event, in order to evaluate it. Has advantage of immediate playback.	Filming evangelism team sharing their faith story with one another. Role playing a committee in progress.	30 mins– 3 hours+
Case study	Small group	Concrete problems which simulate real life events and people, presented to participants for them to work on and from which principles can be derived.	See Case Study 12.	45 mins – 2 hours+
Debrief	Any size	A means of helping people detach themselves from a role they have been asked to play by discussing what it was like and how they felt. The debrief is usually handled by a trainer using questions and answers. An important way of getting people back from a simulated situation to the reality of the present.	See Case Study 19.	30 mins – 1 hour+
Demonstration	Small and medium group	Experienced person shows others how a practical task is done, observers then try the task themselves.	See Case Study 13.	20 mins – 2 hours
Fish bowl	Small group	One group practises or takes part in an experience observed by another group who record their observations. Followed by discussion and sharing of observations.	See Case Study 14.	45 mins – 2 hours

Method	Group size	Description	Example	Time required
Games	Small and medium group	Fun ways of learning new skills or information. May use a board as in *Snakes and Ladders* and *Monopoly*, or role play. Often an element of competition and/or co-operation to increase motivation.	See Case Study 15.	1–2 hours
Human relations exercise	Small group	Experiential exercises that are used to increase people's awareness of themselves or sensitivity to others. Often involve taking part in activities followed by introspective reflection and sharing of observations, feelings, reactions etc.	See Case Study 16.	1½–3 hours
Ice-breakers	Any size	A means of helping people to relax at the start or during a course, a way of helping people mix and develop relationships with others. A means of producing a 'warm' atmosphere on a course.	See Case Study 17.	10 mins – 1 hour
Practical/workshop	Small group	A structured session in which people practise skills – either after demonstration or using step-by-step guides on worksheets.	Practising mime, telling stories. Providing publicity. Preparing a news sheet.	1 hour – day +
Problem-solving exercises	2–3 small group	Real or manufactured situations that may confront trainees are presented (often in written form) for them to solve. Solutions are reached through group discussion.	See Case Study 18.	45 mins – 2 hours

Method	Group size	Description	Example	Time required
Reflection exercises	1–2	Exercises that encourage participants to think back over their own experience and to identify what they already know, to help them to become a resource to others on the course. Also used to help people assess the impact of a training event on their own learning and the effect it will have on their own ministry.	See Case Study 21.	20 mins – 45 mins
Role play	2–3 small group	Acting out real-life situations as a means of practising relationship or communication skills. Participants are usually asked to take on the role of someone else as a means of helping them empathize with the feelings and behaviour of others. The role play is followed by debrief and discussion.	See Case Study 19.	45 mins – 2 hours
Values clarification	1–2 small group	A means of helping people to clarify their own values – the things that are important to them. This is often done by selecting statements from lists of possible values, and is followed by sharing a discussion.	Why have house groups? Participants put in their order of priority statements from a list of possible reasons. This highlights their own feelings, views, attitudes.	30 mins – 1½ hours

Appendix C illustrates how methods can be selected and used at training events.

The following case studies illustrate the use of nine of the methods described above in more detail. Each case study represents one session of a course, not the whole training course. The broader context of the course is described in each case study.

CASE STUDY 12:
Using the **case study** method
on Sunday school leaders' course

Participants: Four experienced Sunday school teachers with some responsibility for Sunday school policy.

Purpose:

The case study is part of a course to help them re-evaluate their work. In this exercise they had to analyse the problems of a fictitious Sunday school and to suggest solutions. This was a means of helping them to develop problem-solving skills for themselves.

Duration:

1 hour.

Description:

The group were given a duplicated pack that contained the following items:

- a breakdown of numbers in the Sunday school by age and sex
- a brief character/personality description of each teacher
- a plan of all the church facilities
- a church timetable for Sunday
- details of specific problems faced, for example (a) the need to integrate children into the church as a whole (b) the need to encourage the use of more relevant teaching methods

Timing:

The group had 30 minutes to study the material, analyse problems and produce solutions. There followed 30 minutes' discussion of their findings and decisions.

Follow-up:

The group were asked to produce a similar analysis of their

own Sunday school and to consider the major problems that needed working at. This was to be completed over a four-week period with a follow-up evening meeting to look at results.

Trainer's role:
To introduce the exercise and explain the group's task, to help them keep to time, to answer questions and queries, to be available to help during the exercise, to conduct the follow-up meeting, asking questions which encouraged them to share what they had learned and to encourage the group to work at the problems they identified in their own Sunday school.

CASE STUDY 13:
Using the **demonstration** method in training people to use an overhead projector

Participants: Five people from very different backgrounds, all potential OHP users – youth worker, Sunday school teacher, preacher, fellowship group leader, baptism class helper. All had little or no experience of using an OHP.

Purpose:
To give skills and confidence in using an OHP and help in knowing when it is an appropriate tool.

Duration:
1½ hours.

Description:
- The trainer briefly explained the way an OHP worked and how it was used.
- He then pointed out all the parts of the machine and their use.
- Participants were allowed 10 minutes to handle the OHP, to look inside, to focus and position.
- The trainer briefly explained the different ways of using an OHP and the ways of producing and using acetates. Acetate samples were shown and produced.

- Participants were asked to list all the ways they might use an OHP in their own work, and then to select one item from their list and to produce an acetate that could be of use in their work. This took 30 minutes.
- Each participant placed his or her acetate on the machine and talked briefly about how he or she would use it.
- The trainer illustrated some techniques in using an OHP to give a talk.
- Participants and trainer brainstormed some of the pitfalls of an OHP and considered how to avoid them.
- Main points were provided on a handout that participants took away.

Follow-up:

Participants were encouraged to use the OHP within the next month and to refer any further queries or problems to the trainer.

Trainer's role:

The demonstration involved a thorough knowledge of the OHP by the trainer. The trainer collected various sample acetates for display. There was time for participants to handle the machine and ask questions.

CASE STUDY 14:
Using the **fish bowl** method in training people to lead a discussion

Participants: A mixed group of people involved in a variety of church activities (home groups, youth leaders, women's group, committee chairpeople) with a wide range of experience. Ten participants.

Purpose:

To improve the skills of leading a discussion.

Duration:

45 minutes to 1 hour.

Description:
The group was divided into two, one containing six members, the other containing four. The group of six were asked to appoint a leader (someone wanting to practise discussion leader skills) and told that they were to be given a topic for discussion and that they would have 10 minutes to reach some concrete conclusions. The second group of four were asked to observe the discussion using a 'prompt' sheet indicating what to look for and describe. The 'prompt' sheet (similar to the one described in Case Study 7) had the following headings under which observations could be recorded:

How is discussion initiated?

What does the leader do to help discussion along at various stages?

What happens during silences?

Describe any feelings portrayed by participants at any stage of the discussion.

Describe anything at any stage that hinders discussion.

How did the discussion end?

Did any group members other than the appointed leader take on particular roles during the discussion?

The discussion group were given a controversial topic to discuss: 'How can the reluctant church be persuaded to accept women in leadership positions?'

Follow-up:
A 30-minute discussion time took place after the fish bowl. The appointed leader was asked to comment on his or her own strengths and weaknesses during the discussion and feedback was given to the leader by others (both those in the discussion group and the observers). Alternative ways of responding as a leader to particular situations were also discussed.

Trainer's role:
- To explain the exercise and its purpose, to ensure that everyone understands
- To observe all that goes on during the discussion, acting as an extra observer

- to control and structure the follow-up discussion, feeding in own observations at the end
- To ensure some summary of discoveries.

CASE STUDY 15:
Using the **simulation game** method in training door-to-door visitors

Participants: A group of thirty-two from the church about to undertake door-to-door visiting as part of an evangelistic campaign being mounted by the church.

Purpose:

To prepare people for some of the reactions they might meet on the doorstep and to practise possible responses.

Duration:

40 minutes.

Description:

A large board hand-drawn like that illustrated below. One board for each eight people (four separate games).

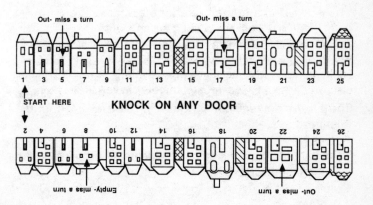

Out- miss a turn   Out- miss a turn

1 3 5 7 9 11 13 15 17 19 21 23 25

START HERE

KNOCK ON ANY DOOR

2 4 6 8 10 12 14 16 18 20 22 24 26

Empty- miss a turn   Out- miss a turn

Players take it in turns to throw the dice and move the required number of houses. At each house where there is someone at home they pick up a 'reaction card' and share their response. The 'reaction cards' describe a variety of types of people, circumstances and questions or comments from the residents (eg 'I'm sorry, we're Roman Catholics', 'Church! You must be joking. You never did anything for me when my wife died', 'Look, I've just come off night shift, so clear off!', 'Oh! I did enjoy the carol service that Christmas'). After the player has responded to the situation, others chip in with alternatives and discussion follows on for a while.

The session is rounded off with the question, 'What can we learn from this game?' Points are written up for all to see.

Trainer's role:
- To explain the exercise
- To keep time
- To structure the discussion and ensure any necessary summary.

CASE STUDY 16:
Using a **human relations exercise** at a course on counselling skills

Participants: Nine people involved in offering pastoral care to others in the church in various situations (visiting the sick, bereavement counselling, general pastoral care). The exercise was run by someone experienced in sensitivity training. The group meet regularly and already have a level of trust and openness.

Purpose:
To strengthen the existing pastoral team by focusing on the way the team worked.

Duration:
1¾ hours.

Description:

The aim of the exercise was explained and participants were given a handout containing the following questions:

1. Describe how you feel about this group, using a colour. Eg, you may choose red because it suggests warmth and comfort.
2. How would you describe your place in this group? Look at the diagram of circles which represents this group and its members. Which circle best represents where you feel you are?

Put the names of the others in the group against any circle that you feel represents where they are in the group.

3. What is the value of this group for you?
4. What else would you like this group to do for you?
5. Is there anything else you could offer this group if given the chance?
6. How could this group help you to be more effective as a counsellor?
7. What would this group need to do to make you trust it more?

Participants were given 20 minutes to think through and fill in the questionnaire. Answers were then shared in pairs (and one threesome) – 20 minutes given to this. During the last 60 minutes, each individual shared his or her answers openly with the whole group, and the group responded by looking at the implications to its own functioning.

When all the participants' feelings had been talked through and any action agreed the session finished with a time of prayer – participants praying for the group and for each other.

Follow-up:

The group agreed to carry out any action needed to make the group more effective.

Trainer's role:

- To anticipate potential reaction to an unfamiliar exercise and to be prepared to explain the point of such an unusual approach; to encourage participation but provide the safety valve so that any who want to opt out of sections of the exercise can do so without feeling a failure
- To introduce and describe the exercise
- To keep time
- To lead the sharing; to ensure that destructive and unhelpful personal comments are not made; to ensure that people can express their feelings and have time to talk about them
- To encourage the formulation of constructive suggestions and helpful actions
- To counsel any with strong feelings that remain at the end of the session.

CASE STUDY 17:
Using an **icebreaker and reflection** exercise
for training welcomers

Participants: A group of twenty people who have volunteered to act as welcomers to newcomers at Sunday services. The twenty are working in groups of four on a rota, one group on duty per week.

Purpose:

This is a first training course and the first time the whole group has met. The aim of this icebreaker is to open the course and help people to feel more relaxed.

Duration:

40 minutes.

Description:

(1) As participants arrived they were asked to wander around the room introducing themselves to anyone they didn't

know and sharing with each person, in turn, their memories of being welcomed into something new (a church, a club, a new job), recalling the good and bad welcome experiences. They were also asked to note anyone who had an experience similar to their own. (20 minutes.)

(2) When the course formally started participants were divided into pairs and asked to list all the good and bad welcome experiences they had heard or shared in the icebreaker and to use these experiences as a basis for listing some do's and don'ts of welcoming newcomers into the church. The pairs work was reported to the whole course and a master list of do's and don'ts were written up on OHP, the course leader adding other principles not identified by pairs. (20 minutes.)

Follow-up:

The training continued with role play etc. helping people to practise skills and consider what exactly was expected of them.

Trainer's role:

- To model what he/she wants of the people on the course, eg participation and sharing of experiences
- To introduce the exercise
- To keep time.

CASE STUDY 18:
Using a **problem-solving** exercise for training youth workers

Participants: A group of eight leaders and potential leaders of youth groups (14+) in the church.

Purpose:

To develop problem-solving skills in dealing with a variety of issues common to the youth work in this particular church.

Duration:
1¼ hours.
Description:
Participants were divided into pairs, and each person given a problem printed on a piece of paper. The participants were to discuss the problems in their pairs. The eight problems in total included:

'Towards the end of the evening's programme, one of the young people in charge of the tuck shop comes to tell you that a five pound note is missing.'

'At the meeting of the planning group (made up of members and leaders) three of the teenage members ask for a showing of an '18' rated film that you know has explicit violence and sex in it.'

'There's a rumpus in one of the side rooms. When you enter, two boys are fighting violently – one is obviously drunk.'

After twenty minutes, pairs had to present their problems and suggested solutions to the rest of the course. The presentations were followed by twenty minutes of general discussion during which alternative solutions were offered.

Trainer's role:
- To introduce the exercise and ensure understanding
- To keep time
- To keep own comments and insights back until near the end
- To draw the session to a conclusion and if necessary to ensure some summary of findings.

CASE STUDY 19:
Using a role play and debriefing exercise for
training those running an old people's lunch club
Participants: All eight helpers at an old people's lunch club held every Thursday in the church hall.

Purpose:

To make them more aware of the problems of handling old people in particular situations.

Duration:

10 minutes role play, 30 minutes debrief.

Description:

Role play. In four groups of two, participants were given the following situation to role play. They were asked to read the situation and decide who would play which role, and then to act it out, playing the role they had chosen as if they were that person.

Situation. One gentleman in his late seventies at first refuses to join the others at the meal table and is now sitting looking at his meal as it gets cold. He has made no move to eat it.

Role 1. You are a member of the lunch club team and have noticed the gentleman in question. He has taken a lot of time to settle. He has never been before.

Role 2. You are in your late seventies. You feel annoyed that you've been forced to come to this club by the matron of the community home where you live. You find it an effort to express yourself and your feelings and can only communicate through your actions of non-co-operation. You are determined never to come again.

Pairs role play at the same time so there is no audience. After 5 minutes the role play is called to a close by the trainer and the trainer leads a debrief.

Debrief. The debrief is a controlled discussion led by the trainer, aimed at getting people to distance themselves from their roles in order to look at the behaviour more objectively and to learn from it. The following questions from the trainer give direction to the discussion:

a) How did *you* actually feel in your role? (Not your *thoughts* or how *others* might feel.)

b) How was the situation handled in your role play?

c) How realistic was your role play?

d) What alternative behaviour could be exhibited by the lunch club worker?

e) What do you learn about the behaviour of some old people from this role play?

Trainer's role:
- To introduce the exercise and ensure understanding
- to keep time
- To lead the debrief and ensure that everyone leaves his or her role behind and can examine what happened objectively.

All these case studies are offered as illustrations of the ways in which methods and the subjects being explored can be brought together when designing a programme. Again the reader should examine Appendix C for further illustrations.

Step 8: Collecting and preparing resources
This could take some time, especially if it involves writing away for materials, seeking advice on who to ask, devising exercises, and preparing handouts, worksheets, and OHP slides.

Step 9: Conducting the course
The trainer's role in conducting a training course is more than that usually associated with the teacher. Like the teacher, the trainer enables the agreed programme to be pursued. The trainer has other vital functions when conducting a course and these are all concerned with creating a climate in which adults can learn.

1. *Creating the right atmosphere*
John comes to the Saturday training course after a busy week at work and leaves his wife frantically

preparing for the visit of parents. Jean is anxious and uncertain if she will cope with anything new. Susan is quite shy and doesn't really know anyone. Peter and Mary if left to their own devices would stick together and not talk to anyone else.

People who attend a course need time to adjust to the training environment. Even if those attending know each other well they need time to become acclimatized.

Instead of diving straight into the training, or even an act of worship or introductory talk, the trainer needs to give people *time* and *help* to prepare for the courses. This is one function of icebreakers. A sample icebreaker has been described in Case Study 16 but they can be designed in any number of ways. Most will contain some of the following elements:

  i) informal mixing of participants so that everyone meets and talks to everyone else

  ii) the chance to talk to others on the understanding that once you hear your own voice in a group you feel more relaxed

  iii) fun and laughter – a tension reliever

  iv) physical contact – touching may be inhibiting to some at first but is a barrier-breaker

  v) movement – around the meeting place, either planned or spontaneous, helps people to feel at home in the environment

  vi) light-hearted sharing of information about themselves, their world, their expectations and fears for the course

  vii) a game to play based loosely on the theme of the course

  viii) ways of beginning to build relationships with others on the course, helping people to feel 'we're in this together' and therefore supported.

This preparation period may take fifteen minutes or an hour but can be time well spent in developing openness to what is to follow.

2. *Encouraging people to learn*

Many Christian adults see learning as a passive activity that simply involves absorbing knowledge or information. Adults have grown used to sitting and receiving information, relying on the skills of the teacher to make the material interesting and understandable. This attitude needs to change because it doesn't encourage translating learning into practice and denies the biblical teaching of our joint responsibility in discipleship – God and man, teacher and learner.

At training events the trainer needs to encourage participants to take their learning seriously, to see that it has practical implications that they must be prepared to face, and to see that they share responsibility for their own learning. One method of encouraging this attitude to learning is to use a **learning contract** at the beginning or even prior to the course.

A learning contract explains what is expected on a course, encourages participation and challenges people to be committed to the results of their training. It also helps all who attend to see that they can play a part in helping each other to learn.

Contracts can be given out for people to read and assent to verbally or can actually be signed by participants prepared to make the commitment. In instances where the idea of contracts seem strange or people resist the idea they can be offered as an option to those who are prepared to make such a commitment.

CASE STUDY 20:
A learning contract

In attending this conference I am willing to:

* *Participate* in sessions and activities as a means of furthering both my own and others' learning.
* *Share* my thoughts, opinions and feelings as honestly and as openly as I feel is appropriate so that others can respond to me in appropriate ways.
* *Set and develop* personal learning goals that I will work at – accepting some responsibility for my own learning.
* *Be prepared* to take risks in exploring ideas, skills, practices and information that are new to me.
* Where necessary *support* others on the conference who are struggling with new ideas, skills, practices, information, etc.
* Help *create* an atmosphere of trust, openness and acceptance in order that others may learn.

Another important means of encouraging people in their learning is through worship. Worship can be an important element of any training event. It can fulfil a number of functions:

  (i) it is a way of acknowledging God's involvement in the training
 (ii) it encourages commitment to what is learned
(iii) it provides a way of responding to God as he equips and empowers us for service.

This acknowledgement and response to God in worship can be an important aid in helping people to change their ideas, attitudes and behaviour.

3. *Sensitivity to people*

Throughout the duration of the course the trainer's role is to remain sensitive and aware of how people are responding to what is happening. People may express needs in a variety of ways:

- Andrew falls asleep in the session after lunch
- Pauline is hurt by something someone said in a group
- Mike is challenged by a role play

Sometimes a group or even the whole course responds in some way:

- The course is covering old ground and people are restless
- A group fails to understand instructions and look lost when asked to get on with the task
- Generally accepted practice is challenged and causes a mixture of anger and bewilderment.

The trainer has to decide what, if anything, to do to cope with the needs he sees expressed by individuals or the whole group during the course. Action could include:

i) changing the pace from intense introspective activities to lighter activities

ii) inserting practical work in pairs after a time of heavy information

iii) explaining the purpose of an exercise again to ensure understanding

iv) using fun or humorous activities to ease the tension after a hard session

v) having a break for refreshments

vi) alternating times of high concentration with times when there is time to relax and not think at all

vii) anticipating negative reactions or resistance to some methods and introducing them sensitively as a means of encouraging participation

viii) changing the nature of a session in order to focus on something new that has arisen.

4. *Helping the transfer of learning*

Those attending external courses may have the greatest problem in transferring what they have experienced on the course to their real work in counselling, youth club, house group, Sunday school, etc. But even home-grown training events which have been specially designed to meet the needs of the people and locality are one step away from reality. On every course, time needs to be given for participants to think through the implications of what they have learned for their real work, and to begin to plan how they will put this learning into action. The group attending the course may be able to act as a support to each other as they try to put learning into practice – as they plan and try to implement changes, or struggle in applying newly acquired values This process can be aided by spending the last minutes of a course (as much as an hour could be allocated to this) encouraging participants to:

a) **reflect** on what they have learned
b) **share** their learning with others
c) **plan** how to use it (again possibly using others on the course to help).

Case Study 21 is a sample exercise to be used at the end of a course. It starts with personal reflection and ends with planning and sharing.

CASE STUDY 21:
A course reflection exercise

1. Think back over all the things you've done on this course – each activity, the discussions, the informal times. Now list all that you've learned that you feel has implications to your

work – new ideas to put into practice, new skills, new resources, new understandings and attitudes.
2. Share your list with others in your group (allow each person 5 minutes in which to share).
3. Now decide what you need to do to put the ideas on your list into effect in your work, decide what obstacles there might be to change (people problems, structure problems, problems in yourself). Decide on one practical thing you could do within the next month that will help you begin to tackle the obstacles *and/or* that will help you begin to take action.
4. Use a partner to help you fill in the table below. They can act as consultant to you and then you to them.

Item to do	Obstacles	First practical step

5. Spend time as a group praying for each other and for your work.

Step 10: Evaluate

At the end of a training event there remains one more important activity – evaluation. Each means of training needs to be evaluated in order to check that it has achieved what it set out to achieve. This is examined in more detail in the next chapter.

THINGS TO DO

1. Use the framework provided in this chapter to plan a training course (evening, day, or weekend) for one area of ministry in your church.
2. If you already run training sessions with groups in your church try out some of the *methods* described in this chapter that are new to you.
3. Using the principles for organizing and running courses outlined in this chapter evaluate any course that has already taken place. Decide what new procedures (if any) you should adopt in the future.

7
The Role and Skills of the Trainer

Who are the trainers in the local church?

Are they trained professionals like the minister, the assistant minister or curate? Are they those with authority like the deacons or elders? Are they the gifted teachers whose ability to preach or give the well-prepared talk is already tested and recognized? Are they those with plenty of experience – the person with twenty years' experience in evangelism, the caterer of twelve years' standing, the parents of eight children?

Or do we need to look for and train a completely new breed of person for a new form of ministry?

Training is certainly a distinct ministry. It isn't the same as teaching but doesn't fit into other traditional church activities. Training combines the communication skills of the traditional teacher with the sensitivity of a good counsellor. As for other areas of ministry, the trainer needs a range of identifiable skills, knowledge and attitudes in order to function effectively. Trainers therefore can be trained.

The trainers in the local church may already have some responsibility. The Sunday school superintendent may be the right person to develop the training programme for the Sunday school team. The house group co-ordinator may be the ideal person to train house group leaders. The experienced evangelist may be ideal as a trainer of others in evangelism.

But these people may not make good trainers. They may be good practitioners, with plenty of knowledge and experience, but have no ability to communicate to others. They may be blinkered and limited by their own experience, they may be insensitive to those being trained and they may be poor at enabling others to develop skills. The dangers of assuming that because someone can do a job they can train others to do it cannot be overstated.

Training often fails in its usefulness because trainers are so concerned with their own agenda and past experiences that they are unable to see the needs or meet the expectations of those being trained.

Training also fails when the trainer makes those being trained dependent on his or her knowledge or abilities. The trainer must be willing to free people to learn for themselves, to find their own way of doing things, to solve their own problems and eventually to be able to work at their own growth and development.

FINDING TRAINERS IN YOUR CHURCH

In looking for potential trainers, what should a church be looking for? Here's a list of skills, gifts and characteristics worth looking out for. Don't limit your search to existing, established leaders – others may have the potential.

• Gifts of discernment and wisdom. Of the gifts described in the New Testament, these seem closest to sensitivity and awareness.

• Concern for other people and a willingness to put others first. Ideally a trainer is a servant who is able to view training as meeting other people's needs and not just passing on his/her own knowledge and experience.

• Ability to communicate with people individually and in groups. This does not mean that people who are good at preaching necessarily make good trainers. A trainer's communication skills are more to do with making themselves understood than they are to do with communicating ideas and information.

• The ability to help others express themselves and look for answers rather than jumping in with advice and ideas all the time.

• Some experience of a particular area of work, such as pastoral counselling, work with teenagers, etc.

• Skills and experience outside the church that are similar to those described in the next section of this chapter, 'The skills of the trainer'.

Looking for potential is one means of finding the trainers in the church. A more thorough approach is to identify the major skills and roles of the trainer and to use this analysis to train trainers. In the next section we do just that.

THE SKILLS OF THE TRAINER

In a book that has emphasized the importance of developing skills for ministry it is important that space is given to examining the skills required by those who take on a training role. The eight basic skills considered in the rest of this section are fundamental to the trainer.

1. The ability to listen

Listening is a more complex skill than many realize. It certainly doesn't come naturally to everyone. It involves being able to give full attention to what others are saying in order to understand what they really mean. Listening involves hearing the words that are spoken, being aware of the feelings underlying them and interpreting the message the 'speaker' intends to communicate. Listening includes observing the speaker's behaviour, which can help to convey the meaning of the message. It can also involve the listener in asking questions to check that the message is understood.

• A trainer designing a course must *listen* to those being consulted in order to understand their needs. An over-enthusiastic trainer may read his own interests into the consultation process if he does not give full attention when listening.

• A supervisor has to *listen* to the person she is supervising as they reflect on their last training experience. This listening should give her a clear picture of what happened and how it affected the person being trained. Listening should provide the supervisor with the understanding she needs to help the trainee in his or her development.

• During a training course the trainer needs to be able to *listen* to questions, so that any answers he or she gives are addressed to the needs being expressed in the question. In a group discussion the trainer needs to be *listening* to all contributions in order to facilitate a worthwhile exchange of views, or the completion of some task.

Good listening is a discipline that involves sensitivity on the part of the trainer. Listening skills can be developed with practice. They can also be improved with increased awareness of self and others.

2. *The ability to observe*
This involves observing people in action and being able to note what they are doing and its effects. Essential to observation is an understanding of the nature of the task – what is meant to happen and what the outcome ought to be. Knowing what to expect helps the observer make sense of what they see.

• The trainer *observes* the apprentice house group leader taking on their first piece of real responsibility.

• A supervisor joins in the youth club discussion to *observe* the youth leader working at her discussion-leading skills recently developed through a training course.

• At a conference the trainer *watches* participants as they take part in a practical session to ensure they understand the task.

• At a course a trainer *observes* a group involved in a human relations exercise; these observations will be shared along with contributions from those who took part in the discussion that follows.

3. *The ability to reflect and help others reflect*
Reflection is the way people begin to make sense of their experiences. It usually involves looking back to something that happened as a way of trying to understand it and consider its relevance and application. A trainer has to be able to reflect on things observed during training. Through their ability to reflect, trainers should also be able to help learners

reflect on their own experiences. Reflection can be aided by asking questions that help:

i) recalling what actually happened

ii) recalling feelings about what happened

iii) exploring current feelings about what happened

iv) interpreting and evaluating the experience (the value of what happened, what was learned and how it was or will be utilized).

● Trainers need to be able to *reflect* on the experiences they have when training – whether through running courses, acting as supervisors or aiding an apprentice.

● Supervision and apprenticeship trainers have to encourage trainees to *reflect* on past training experiences.

● On a training course *reflection* is used to help participants recall and learn from their past experiences or as a means of getting the most out of an experience actually given to people on the course.

● A trainer uses *reflection* as one means of helping to evaluate a training event.

One of the hardest elements of reflection for many people is recalling and expressing their feelings. The trainer should be able to identify and describe their own feelings as a means of helping others do the same.

Reflection is in many respects a simple process but is often poorly utilized by people. As a skill it can be developed by being aware of the process and finding time to practise it consciously.

4. *The ability to organize*

A trainer should be able to design a programme using information from a variety of sources (see chapter 3). He or she should also be able to bring together a range of resources – people, materials, equipment etc. – and to see that they combine in the most effective way for those receiving training. As well as organizing programmes the trainer should also be able to 'organize' people – not in a patronizing or paternalistic way, but in order to provide a level of sensitivity and structure that frees them to learn.

5. *The ability to help others learn*
So much of the discipling in the church is teacher-centred. Training is essentially learner-centred. In other words, it is concerned that the learner takes something away from the training experience that will be helpful in their work. This involves the trainer in understanding how adults learn and the potential obstacles to their learning. It also requires the trainer to be continually sensitive to the needs and feelings of the person being trained. Trainers often have to put aside their own pet interests, areas of expertise and hobby horses so that the trainee can be helped. The following are some of the ways a trainer may need to be aware of trainees' needs in order to help them to learn:

● by including a variety of training methods in the design of a course

● by sitting back and listening before making comments of their own

● by using discovery methods, that are not as directive as a talk or lecture, but have a deeper impact on a trainee's learning.

The ability to help people learn involves being able to use a variety of training methods each of which can, to some extent, be gained through practice. It also involves knowledge of adulthood itself and a sensitivity to others.

6. *The ability to build trust and openness*

Adult learners feel secure and more open to trying out new things when they trust the trainer. A trainer develops trust in a number of ways:

i) by showing warmth and real concern for the people being trained

ii) by encouraging and affirming those under training in a way that isn't patronizing

iii) by being learners themselves and showing that they are open to learning from those being trained

iv) by being honest

v) by clearly explaining what is being done and why

vi) by showing sensitivity to those involved in training and caring in practical ways for those who need support

vii) by their own behaviour and through the way they design the training.

● the use of an appropriate icebreaker at the start of a training event can help course members to *trust* one another.

● the apprenticeship trainer who encourages and accepts negative feedback of his or her own practice helps to build a bond of *trust* with the apprentice.

● the trainer can gain *trust* when he or she provides some escape clause for those who find an exercise particularly difficult, eg 'If you want to share your answers to the exercise with others in your group do . . . if you prefer to remain silent and listen to the others then feel free to do that . . .'

7. *The ability to give and receive feedback*

Feedback involves giving some objective information about a person's behaviour and the way it affects others. It must be clearly distinguished from praise and criticism:

Praise: 'John, you did really well, it was a great session.'

Criticism: 'I didn't like the way you did that. It wasn't up to your usual standard.'

These tend to be subjective, often offered from feelings of satisfaction or displeasure and intended to *promote feelings* in the one who receives them.

Feedback, on the other hand, is meant to encourage a *thinking response*, as distinct from an emotional one. It has the one aim of aiding the growth and development of the person on the receiving end.

Someone undergoing training may well ask questions like, 'How am I doing?' 'Is this right?' or 'What can I do to improve?' Even if these questions aren't actually posed they need to be answered if the value of any training is to be assessed. Giving and receiving feedback is one way of answering these questions and providing some measurement of effectiveness.

Preparing people for feedback

There may seem to be a fine line between praise or criticism and real feedback. In order to ensure that feedback is received in the right way it should be offered after careful preparation:

i) In the early stages of training, feedback should be accepted by all parties as part of the training process. Where a learning contract is used it could be written in as a formal agreement, otherwise it can be acknowledged verbally.

ii) The nature of feedback should be understood by everyone involved. It should be clear that it is not to be offered as criticism or praise but as a means of promoting the development of someone's ministry. It should be given with sensitivity and a concern for how it will be received.

iii) Feedback should be given in the context of trusting relationships where people feel comfortable with openness and honesty.

iv) Feedback should be given as soon after the event as possible and at a time when it will be helpful to the receiver.

v) Those giving feedback need some idea of the nature of the activity or role in which the person being trained is involved. They need some understanding of the skills/behaviour required so that they can focus their feedback on the important areas.

Giving feedback

i) **Describe** *behaviour/actions. Do not* **evaluate** *them.*
'When John asked you a question you listened and looked away as if you didn't want to answer.'
OR
'You stood in front of the overhead projector at the end of your talk so the visual aid wasn't visible.'
NOT
'It was unhelpful to John when you didn't answer his question. I think you must have been afraid of showing your ignorance.'

ii) *Describe the* **effects** *of the action/behaviour on others.*
'The children were very restless during the last section of the story you told.'
OR
'When you introduced that session I found myself really wanting to take part. That was an indication of how secure I felt.'
NOT
'You were rather laboured when you told that story.'

iii) **Check** *your own perceptions of what happened as part of feedback.*
'When you were trying to encourage John to share his

problem you appeared very nervous as if you weren't sure what to say. Is that right?'

iv) *Be* **specific**.

Don't make vague general statements like:

'You dominated from the front!'

Instead, relate such observations to specific behaviour:

'When you handled the question-and-answer time, there was a lot of input from you and little time for people to ask questions or follow your comments up.'

v) *Describe* **feelings**.

If you, as trainer, were on the receiving end of the trainee's leadership at some time during a training session, describe your own *feelings* during the experience. If not, describe your perception of the *feelings* of those who were involved.

'I felt nervous when you kept encouraging Jan to take part in the discussion. She seemed very embarrassed.'

OR

'The committee seemed to get quite excited when you encouraged them to try out that new method of problem-solving. They really appeared to be supporting you.'

The examples of feedback given above all relate to training which involved working with other groups of people. Feedback can, however, be offered as a result of any training.

● The producer of the church magazine or news-sheet can be given feedback on their work.

● The catering team can be given feedback after a major function which involved them in trying out some new ways of working.

● The apprentice house group leader receives feedback after their first attempt to lead the group.

● The new pre-school leader receives feedback

from the person acting as supervisor after telling his first story.

- A training course member receives feedback from another course member on their role play of a counselling situation.

Feedback can be given by the trainer, an outside observer or a fellow trainee.

It is an appropriate means to growth and change for the experienced as well as the beginner. Where teams of people work on the same activity the offering and receiving of feedback can be an invaluable means of cementing team relationships. If experienced team members show they are as willing and open to receive feedback as anyone else, an atmosphere of trust and a continual openness to growth and change can be nurtured.

Trainers themselves must also be willing to receive feedback on their own role. This can come from the people they are training. The trainer needs to be seen to be asking the questions:

'How did I do?'

'What effect did my action have on you as the learner?'

'How can I improve?'

This has two effects:

i) it enables the trainer to evaluate his work

ii) it acts as a model of openness to learning for those being trained.

Responding to feedback

Giving feedback is not the same as demanding a change in the person at the receiving end. Feedback may in fact be describing good practice which is then reinforced. When the feedback focuses on behaviour that could be unhelpful the decision to change remains in the hands of the person on the receiving end. People may respond to feedback in a number of ways:

   i) they may receive it, agree with it, but prefer not to act on it

   ii) they may feel the feedback is wrong, based on a wrong perception, and they may therefore challenge it

   iii) they may receive it and make changes as a result. Information given in feedback is 'raw' – the result of observation and perception. If it is free of judgements the receiver can reflect on it and make his own decision about what to do with it. This is an important part of the feedback process which needs to be made clear to all who give and receive.

8. *An awareness of self*

Trainers need to be able to look critically at their own behaviour and performance. This healthy introspection should enable them to know themselves well – their own personalities, strengths, weaknesses, limitations and the way they tend to react in particular situations. It should include an awareness of how they relate to others and the blocks they have in relationships or in communicating with others.

Such self-knowledge can ensure that the trainer is a real servant to those being trained.

● A trainer who knows that he or she feels personally threatened and gets anxious when asked difficult questions is able to prevent those feelings from becoming a block to the curious, questioning trainee.

● The supervisor who knows that he or she talks too much and doesn't listen enough can try to monitor and control this unhelpful behaviour during a supervision session.

● The trainer who is not very hot on accurate

observation may bring someone in to help observe a trainee at work.

- A trainer who is aware and open about the influences of his own spiritual journey can become sensitive to the struggles and encouragements in the lives of others and can help people to understand the link between spiritual growth and the development of skills.

- The trainer who knows that she works better with small groups than medium or large groups may bring someone else in to take the larger group session.

- The trainer who knows that his ability to use an overhead projector leaves much to be desired may choose to work at this skill and undergo training himself.

Self-awareness can be developed by asking for feedback from others at a training course or even by videoing the trainer at work and examining the recording.

Trainers can also improve their self-understanding by working in a team, with a partner or by using their own supervisor. When trainers know themselves well, they should be open to learning themselves, both in relation to skills and to their spiritual development.

9. A sensitivity to other people

Sensitivity is a gift that some possess and others have to develop. It is an essential training skill and whether it comes naturally or has to be worked at it can be developed and sharpened up in everyone.

Sensitivity involves reading other people's reactions, words and behaviour in order to understand how they are feeling. The trainer needs this sensitivity so that he can do what is necessary to help people in their growth and development in their work for God. As a result of correctly interpreting people's feelings a trainer may choose to act in one of any number of ways – supporting, confronting, encouraging, exploring, affirming, offering feedback, ignoring, questioning, checking their perception, reflecting, etc.

• The *sensitive* trainer counselling others about the content of a training event will see some of the needs that are not expressed but which underlie the words.

• The *sensitive* supervisor is aware of the feelings of the person being supervised.

• At the training course the trainer *senses* the mood of those taking part.

• Although the apprentice is saying: 'Everything went well, I feel confident', the trainer sees that their body language is communicating the reverse.

• A trainer using a human relations exercise is sensitive to the person showing signs of stress, or the person trying gently to sabotage the whole exercise, and acts in the way he or she feels is appropriate to deal with it.

THE ROLES OF THE TRAINER

The description of the *skills* of the trainer described in the last section is one way of building up a picture of the trainer. A second helpful aid is to clarify the different *roles* trainers need to adopt at various stages of training. Six roles are described below:

1. Model
Modelling is a very powerful way of learning whether we realize and acknowledge it or not. Most of us, during our lives, adopt methods of behaving that we

have experienced in other people who have special significance for us. We may cook certain things in the way our mother or father cooked them, some preachers emulate the style of other respected preachers they have seen and heard, our attitude to church leadership may be modelled on the experience of leadership we had in an earlier church, our teaching and learning may be modelled on the experience of these activities during college training. The essence of modelling is that usually it happens without our realizing it.

Whether they like it or not, trainers become models to those they train. The trainer leading a session on communication will pass on as much by the *way* she herself communicates as through the message of her words or the exercises she uses. The design of a training course acts as a model of good or bad organization and may either support or undermine the actual content of the course. During sensitivity training the sensitivity of the trainer will be as significant to those on the course as the actual training they do.

Trainers need to be aware that whenever they work with an individual or a group, modelling could be a powerful means by which people learn, for good or ill! Some of the dangers of modelling have been explored in chapter 4. There are times, however, when the trainer intentionally acts as a model of a particular form of behaviour. When this is done the trainer can have more control over the effects of modelling on those being trained. Modelling as a means of training can be used in all sorts of situations including the following:

● *Demonstrating how to use a computer.* Any demonstration should reflect good practice – in demonstrating the use of a computer the sequence of operations need to be communicated clearly and should mirror what the person being trained will need to do to use the computer.

● *Training people in developing relationships with others*. Developing relationship skills in those who work in youth clubs, with children or on committees could involve a level of modelling. The trainer ensures that the way he or she treats people on the training course reflects what he or she feels constitutes good relationship-building behaviour. If the trainer is encouraging sensitivity, listening, patience, concern, and valuing as important elements of building a relationship the trainer should demonstrate these aspects of behaviour with the people on the course.

● *Apprenticeship training*. Modelling is often a major element of this type of training and has already been covered in some detail in chapter 4.

● *Training in leading a group*. In small group training a trainer may mirror the functions and behaviour of a small group leader with the training group themselves. Such behaviour may involve listening to what trainees have to say, clarifying different people's contributions by asking questions, encouraging and affirming people on the course, and intervening in exercises and projects set for the trainers only when necessary.

● *Training those who teach adults*. In training people who teach adults the trainer may design the course as a model of good adult education and learning – allowing participation, a variety of methods, help for those who find learning on the course difficult, and so forth.

Modelling has a number of implications for the trainer:

i) The need to be aware of the way they work as a trainer. This awareness includes the way they behave and react to people on courses. If a trainer is aware of his or her own values in training (ie the attitudes and practices that they feel are important and would like to see others emulate), they can assess how well they themselves demonstrate these values in the way they train others. This may indicate discrepancies between a trainer's values and their way of working, and point to changes they need to make if they are to become models of good behaviour. A trainer who feels strongly that house group leaders should value *all* contributions made during a discussion time in their house groups should be alert to the way they themselves handle the contributions of those on the leaders' training course.

ii) The need to take special care in designing training in which they intentionally set themselves up as models. They will need to know how the good practice they were trying to model was understood by those being trained – did it come across in the way the trainer intended? Where modelling is intentionally used the trainer should find ways of discovering what trainees actually learned from the experience. This can be done to some extent by reviewing and discussing the activity with the trainees.

iii) The need to make trainees more aware of the way modelling occurs in teaching and training. They should be alerted to the dangers of unwittingly copying someone else and encouraged to reflect on what they have learned from training and to evaluate its effect on them.

2. Facilitator

In training *adults* it is important to recognize that people being trained bring with them:

- their own experience of an activity or ministry –

perhaps from being on the receiving end, or because they've been active in that area of work for many years

• the God-given gifts, talents, abilities that they possess before they undergo any form of training

• their own experience of life – relationships, behaviour, situations – that may have a bearing on the work for which they are being trained.

Training involves harnessing these resources so that people can learn from their own past experiences, can discover their own inbuilt resources, and can share with their peers and learn from each other. Training also involves creating experiences that the trainees can learn from. Having practised using a film projector or leading a small group they can then reflect on the experience and learn from it.

In both these situations the trainer's role is to help the learner share what they have experienced and to make sense of it. In this role the trainer isn't feeding the learner with information and may spend less time talking than the learner. This is facilitation and is a key role of anyone who trains adults.

It is often the hardest role for the 'expert' to take on. If someone who has been an evangelist for years is training others in evangelism, the natural inclination is to tell the trainees how to do it best. This is not facilitation.

The value of facilitation is that it helps learners to discover answers for themselves, to find ways of doing things that will work for them. The end product may be a greater depth of learning and more confidence in getting the job done than through simply being told.

Facilitation is a form of *non-directive* training. The trainer leads from the back, encouraging and enabling rather than telling. It is often distinguished from *directive* training, where the trainer has a more dominant role of informing those being trained. Both approaches to training have a part to play, but in many ways facilitation requires more skill.

- The facilitator works at the pace of the learner.
- The facilitator may initiate an experience/activity/discussion but then allows it to take its own course as far as possible.
- The facilitator encourages learning to take place by providing some structure to the discussion or to the project, but doesn't dominate by feeding in his or her own ideas all the time.
- The facilitator has to be sensitive to what is happening in an exercise or discussion so that he or she can do or say the things that will help it along.
- The facilitator often holds back her own ideas or observations to the end. Instead she waits for those who are learning to discover things themselves and only makes her own contributions if important areas are missed.

The trainer takes on the facilitator role when:

- acting as a supervisor, encouraging someone else to make sense of their most recent experiences. The supervisor has no information to give; he encourages the trainee to recall events, interpret what happened, reflect on her own feelings and reactions. The supervisor may feed in his own ideas and observations only after the trainee has exhausted her own reflections.
- leading a discussion (after a role play or exercise or as a means of exploring an issue). The trainer may introduce the topic and use some means of stimulating discussion, but after that he allows the discussion to flow freely within the group. When the trainer contributes to the group it may be to share his own views and ideas on the topic, but as often as not it will

be to enable the group to function better, eg by encouraging people to listen to each other, ensuring contributions are fully understood, enabling the less articulate to get a word in, preventing the over-talkative from monopolizing the group, suggesting that the group summarize its findings, keeping time for the group.

● Using a role play. The trainer may explain the purpose of the exercise, give out instructions and start the role play off. After that the trainer allows the action to take place, stopping it at the appropriate place and encouraging discussion of what happened, how people felt, and what was learned.

3. Designer

Training needs to be planned and the trainer acts as designer when helping to plan the content and methods to be used. Training design involves discovering the training needs, agreeing the means of training to be used and then bringing together resources, people, and programmes to meet those original needs.

● A supervisor and apprenticeship trainer act as designer when they work with the people being trained to plan a programme for their learning experiences (identifying the knowledge/skills/attitudes needed for the job, agreeing when and how to focus on different elements when they are on the job).

● In preparing for a training course a trainer acts as designer from the moment of initial consultation through to the final evaluation of the course.

Design requires the ability to examine all the different elements involved in training and to put them together in the best way to help people achieve their goals as learners.

4. Builder

The trainer will on occasions be required to build a framework into which people can fit their experiences, skills and knowledge so that they make more sense. The framework may involve helping people to understand the theory behind what they are doing or to see the organizational structure into which they fit. The aim of *building* is to promote greater understanding. It is usually achieved by offering explanation or through illustrated talks and group discussion. It helps people to grasp the principles, models or theories underlying the task or ministry.

The trainer acts as builder when:

• encouraging trainees to look at the biblical principles underlying their particular ministry. During a counselling course, for example, the trainer may include some exploration of the biblical doctrines of personhood and wholeness as a framework in which counsellors can understand and practise their skills.

• painting a broad canvas as an introduction to training in a specific area of work. During a training course for preachers, the trainer may discuss the complexities of the discipling process so that the preachers see their own work as just one activity which is part of a much broader process.

• explaining the theory behind the practice. When training leaders of small groups in the church the trainer may follow a practical exercise on 'how small groups function' with an examination of some of the theories of group development.

5. Resource person

Resources are all those things that help the training process. Trainers need information about resources that will help them to design and conduct training

activities for different groups of people. Resources include:
- people with special skills and knowledge that they can call on
- training exercises that they can use and adapt
- filmstrips or videos that they can use on a course
- handouts to back up training sessions

They also need to know of resources that will be directly helpful to trainees:
- background reading – books, magazines, articles, etc.
- outside courses to attend.

The trainer acts as a resource person to others whenever he recommends a book, suggests a source of further information, or links someone with needs to someone with appropriate experience and expertise. To act as a resource person the trainer has to become a collector and storer of information. Some amass this store in their heads and others prefer filing systems, computers and resource libraries.

6. *Evaluater*

Any stage of training is incomplete until it has been evaluated. In evaluating training the trainer and trainees ask a number of questions about the design of the training, the trainer's role and the outcome of the training:

- Was the training designed in the most effective way to aid those involved?
- Did the trainer carry out his or her role in the most effective way?
- Did the training achieve what it was intended to achieve?

In order to answer these questions information has to be collected from:

i) *those on the receiving end of the training*

The trainer may help participants to assess the value of the training for themselves. The trainer may also use participants to help in his or her own evaluation. The trainer can encourage evaluation by guiding participants to reflect on the training soon after it has happened, perhaps as the last supervisory session or at the end of a training course. The reflection may be encouraged through use of a questionnaire (see Case Study 22).

Evaluation can also be carried out some months after a particular stage of training has been completed. Six months after a training course, participants may be asked to identify the long-term effects of the training on their work, and to specify areas of future training need.

Evaluating training over a period of time gives a much more accurate indication of the value of training than a one-off evaluation. Many people who leave a course or finish an apprenticeship may be excited and enthusiastic as a result of their training but after six months in the 'real work' discover big gaps in their skills, knowledge or attitudes, and on reflection realize that very little of their training has been put into action.

The following case study indicates some of the questions that trainees can be asked in order to help evaluate. Questions are asked in a number of different ways purely to illustrate variety. It may be less confusing to stick to just one or two ways on an actual questionnaire.

CASE STUDY 22:
General evaluation questionnaire
To be filled in by participants after participating in a training activity.

1. Which of *your* expectations and needs were met by the training? (Please be specific.)

2. How helpful was each session? (Place an X on the line to show the value of each session for you.)

	extremely helpful	of no use
a) Session on leadership	_____	
b) Practical session	_____	
c) Exploration of biblical principles	_____	
d) Group discussion	_____	
e) Question and answer time	_____	

3. Which (if any) parts of the training did you find of little use? Put a tick in any relevant column to show why.

	hard to understand	not relevant to my work	too elementary	covered before	other (please specify)
Session 1					
Session 2					
Session 3					
Session 4					
Session 5					

4. How interesting/helpful did you find the methods? Do not evaluate the *content* of the sessions – just the effect of the *methods* used. Cross out whatever does not apply.

Opening exercise   interesting/uninteresting
                             helpful/unhelpful

Group discussion   interesting/uninteresting
                             helpful/unhelpful

Role play	interesting/uninteresting
	helpful/unhelpful
Small group game	interesting/uninteresting
	helpful/unhelpful
Talk	interesting/uninteresting
	helpful/unhelpful
Worship	interesting/uninteresting
	helpful/unhelpful
Bible study	interesting/uninteresting
	helpful/unhelpful
Visit	interesting/uninteresting
	helpful/unhelpful

5. As a result of this training what will you do? (Mention ideas you will use, behaviour you will try out, new skills you will use, knowledge you will utilize, attitude changes you will work at, etc.)

6. What training needs that you hoped would be tackled have been left untouched?

7. As a result of this training can you identify further training you would like? (Please specify.)

8. Any other comments

---

ii) *outside observers*
A more objective evaluation comes from outside observers. They are able to view the training in a more detached way, as they have nothing at stake. The observer may sit in on the training and watch without participating, and may observe the results of the training as the trainees put their learning into practice. The outside observer will need some knowledge of the purpose of the course and an understanding of the nature of training.

iii) *trainer evaluation*
The trainer can make a subjective assessment of the training from his or her own point of view. Trainers will try to assess their own 'performance', the way training was designed, and the outcomes for those on the receiving end. The trainer's own intuitive feelings about the course can be enhanced by making video recordings during the training which can be viewed and analysed when training has been completed.

When information about the course has been collected, the trainer has to make judgements about its effectiveness. In identifying strengths and weaknesses the trainer can improve future decisions about training.

In any evaluation the trainer must return to the original objectives (or purposes) that were identified and which the training was meant to achieve. (See chapter 3 and Case Study 23 below.)

CASE STUDY 23:
Evaluating a course for a drama group

At the end of this course those taking part should:

1. be more confident and effective using mime techniques
2. have a greater understanding of the place of drama in Christian teaching
3. know how to warm up in preparation for any drama presentation
4. know how to read and interpret a drama script

The course was evaluated by:

1. asking participants to talk about what they got out of the course immediately it was over and relating this to the objectives above
2. observing their next performance in relation to the objectives set for the course
3. asking participants to reflect on the course – what they felt about its long-term value

---

If the objectives have not been achieved the trainer may come to one or more of the following conclusions:

- the objectives were wrong (incorrectly identified, incorrectly expressed by participants)
- the means, or methods, of training were inappropriate
- the training was badly designed (wrong combination of methods, too long, too short, too complicated)
- the trainer's role was inappropriate (too directive, not directive enough)

DEVELOPING TRAINERS IN YOUR CHURCH

The potential for developing trainers will vary from church to church and situation to situation. Here we will survey a range of possibilities that could help to meet the needs of small church and large church alike.

The training co-ordinator
Larger churches with scope for specialist ministries and small churches with suitably gifted people may see the need for one or more specialist trainers. These might be people with responsibility to oversee the church's training programme in all areas of ministry. Their work could include: assessing training needs, finding resources for training (themselves, other trainers, materials, external courses, etc), designing training programmes, keeping a training resource library, etc. Such people could be trained using material in this book and through 'training the trainer' courses run by outside agencies.

The ministry specialist
Someone already involved in an area of work could be given responsibility for training others in that area. These people would need to be selected not because of their status or even their experience, but because of their potential as trainers of others. The person might be, for example, the leader of the pastoral team or a member of it. Their role would be to see that a training programme for new and experienced leaders was developed, carried out and evaluated. They could be responsible for collecting training resources related to their area of ministry. In this way some areas of church life may be supported by trainers and others may not.

The occasional trainer

Where specialists are not appropriate a church may look for those who could offer limited training over short periods of time. Examples might include someone involved in an area of work who could act as trainer to an apprentice for three months or so, or a person with the ability to act as supervisor to one or two new leaders in the church. Again, these people would benefit from developing training skills relevant to the nature of their training responsibility.

The training team

The roles of the trainer which we looked at earlier in this chapter do not have to be fulfilled in one person but may be taken on by different people in the church. Training resources could be collected by the person who looks after the church bookstall or library. Someone with little training skill could act as encourager – seeing that training is on the agenda of the church council or of the various groups within the church.

• Someone who has vast experience in one area of ministry might team up with someone else in the church who understands how adults learn, or who is involved in training outside the church, to design training for church members.

• A good teacher might work alongside someone who is good at using role play, games and human relations exercises to produce a training session.

Whatever route a church takes in developing a training ministry and equipping people to be trainers, there needs to be some recognition that training is distinct from other activities, requires some specialist skills and knowledge, and that trainers benefit from being trained.

THINGS TO DO

1. Identify those in your church with the potential to train others.
2. Use the skills/knowledge/attitudes listed below to identify strengths and weaknesses amongst those who already have a training role. Invite them to work at areas of need:

Skills
Ability to listen
Ability to observe
Ability to reflect on experience
Ability to organize
Ability to help others learn
Ability to build trust and openness
Ability to give and receive feedback
Self-awareness
Sensitivity to others

Knowledge
Church structures into which ministry fits
Some knowledge of activity for which they are training
How adults learn
Stages of adulthood and how these affect people
Resources available to support training
A range of training methods
Understanding of how groups function
Understanding the nature of the church
Relevant biblical knowledge
Understanding the nature of training

Attitudes
Openness to learning themselves
Concern for people and their growth
Enthusiasm for training
Willingness to be vulnerable
Willingness to be open and honest
Desire to release the potential in others

8
Training Resources

DEVISE YOUR OWN TRAINING

If you decide to design and conduct your own training you may still require resources from outside your own church. Here are some of the ways in which you might seek help and support:

1. Call in a consultant. Invite someone to help you with the overall plan of your training programme – someone who can help you to develop principles and models that are appropriate for your needs and that you can then use to fill in the details. A good consultant will do a great deal of questioning and probing before offering advice. Be careful of those who want to tell you how to do it before they've discovered in detail your situation, motives and needs. Before making contact with a consultant you will need to do some thinking yourself and have some ideas and plans ready.

2. Use packaged training courses. A number of D.I.Y. training courses are available from Christian agencies. Take care as you choose these – be sure that they are going to meet your needs. Don't let the package dictate the training. Decide first what your

training needs are, then find the package that best meets those needs. Before using the course decide how you want to adapt it. Be prepared to spend some time working through the material, rejecting some parts and adapting others so that it becomes a course that you feel happy with. Beware of training packages that are just glorified teaching courses – if they don't have a practical element they may not really help your leaders develop the skills to do the job. Also beware of training packages that are totally inflexible – it is very rare that you will find material that just suits your needs without some adapting.

3. Use other materials. Books, videos and filmstrips not intended as training courses in themselves can be used to aid your training. They may be used as resources from which you can extract useful training exercises. You may use them as part of a course to stimulate discussion or to provide problems to be solved. You could use some material as back-up homework or as a course reader. Remember these all offer passive means of learning and do not in themselves provide practical training.

Make resources available to those with responsibility in the church. A library of books, articles, and even videos will make distance training material readily available for any leader who wants to work at a particular issue related to their work. A useful way of classifying this material is by *ministry* – evangelism training, small group work, worship leadership, preaching, etc. and by *skills* – using an OHP, listening skills, communication skills, etc.

4. Use outside trainers. Bring in people with training skills to help in those areas where you need special assistance. Be prepared to brief outsiders in some detail and make sure they are coming to meet your

needs rather than just fulfil their own agenda. When you are considering how long the trainer should have, build in time for him or her to get to know those being trained so that some sort of rapport can be developed before the real object of the training is addressed.

Remember, experts in particular fields do not always make good trainers. They may have a proven record of success in their own situation – but this doesn't guarantee that they can communicate with others *or*, more importantly, that they can help others to learn ways of doing things that are appropriate to a different situation.

You may need to spend time with an outside trainer thinking through the methods they are to use and the ways they will ensure that what they do is relevant to your situation.

GOING OUTSIDE FOR TRAINING

The advantages and disadvantages of going elsewhere for training have been covered in chapter 6. When you do decide to go elsewhere then remember to check the programme that is offered to see that it meets some of your needs.

People attending courses away from their own church often complain of the problems they experience when they return. These can be overcome to some extent by:

i) sending people away in teams so that the whole group goes through the same training experience and can reflect on it together. They can then support one another in putting their learning into practice when they return.

ii) appointing an *ad hoc* supervisor for those who go

on a course. Someone who can spend time with those who have been away, helping them to reflect on what they have learned and to apply it to their own work. The supervisor may provide support during the early days as leaders try to put their training into practice.

iii) being sensitive to the potential problem caused when people have an experience not shared by others. A group coming back from a training course may be excited and enthusiastic for change, while those who have not shared the experience may fail to understand or appreciate what has happened. Either group may have feelings of anxiety, threat, anger, frustration or resentment. One way to facilitate a more positive reaction is to encourage those who are returning to think through (a) how they will communicate what they have learned, (b) to whom they will communicate it, (c) with what possible effect and (d) what potential obstacles to change may be created.

TRAINING COSTS MONEY

Remember training costs money. If you do it all yourself the costs of your time and the materials you use will be hidden and probably considered unimportant. Buying or hiring training resources such as videos or training packs will require real money! Using outside trainers or consultants, or sending people on courses organized by training agencies, will cost even more. When the church begins to take training seriously it needs to give it a place in the church's budgets and finances.

RESOURCES GUIDE

The resources listed below are categorized by ministry. Space permits only selected items to be included. The items listed include agencies offering advice, materials and training courses. The books, videos, etc. may be designed for church use or originate from non-Christian agencies. All materials need to be carefully examined and adapted for use in the local situation.

General interest to trainers

1. Books/AVA/magazines etc.

All Are Called: Towards a Theology of the Laity (Church Information Office, 1985)

Encyclopedia of Management Development Methods by A. Huczynski (Gower, 1983)

Go and Make Apprentices by P. Vogel (Kingsway, 1986)

A Handbook of Training Management by K. Robinson (Kogan Page, 1985)

Human Relations Development by C. Gazda et al (Allyn & Bacon, 1977)

Know How to Give a Five-Minute Talk by Lance Pierson (Scripture Union, 1984)

Know How to Use an Overhead Projector by Stephen Clark (Scripture Union, 1985)

Know How – Video by David Lazell (Scripture Union, 1984)

Live and Learn by G. Claxton (Harper & Row, 1984) – explores ways we learn from life

Making Adult Disciples by Anton Baumohl (Scripture Union, 1984) – the way adults learn and its application to the church

Planning Your Own Training Programme by Liz Hogarth
    & D. Grisbrook (NCVYS, 1985)

Reflection: Turning experience into learning ed. D. Boud,
    R. Keogh, D. Walker (Kogan Page, 1985)

The Skills of Human Relations Training by L. Roe (Gower,
    1985)

The Skills of Training by L. Roe (Gower, 1983)

A Strategy for the Church's Ministry by J. Tiller (Church
    Information Office, 1983)

Supervision in Youth Work by J. Tash (YMCA, 1984)

Training for Communication by J. Adair (Gower, 1973)

Training Digest – bulletin from Scripture Union's
    Training Unit, published three times a year with
    details of training courses, articles and resource
    information of interest to those involved in adult
    education and training in the local church.

2. *Agencies*

Denominational agencies usually offer resources,
advice and personal help to those with denominational affiliation in training their leaders. Contact
denominational headquarters.

Higher education institutions – technical colleges,
polytechnics, universities, community schools – often
have extramural departments offering training
courses for adults. Short courses at reasonable costs.
Contact local college for details.

Industrial/management training agencies offer
courses for trainers who want to learn to train. These
have an industrial bias but this does not invalidate
them. Costs are usually very high.

Such agencies include:

BACIE (British Association for Commercial and
    Industrial Education), 16 Park Crescent, London
    W1N 4AP

Guardian Business Services, 119 Farringdon Road, London EC1R 3DA

Institute of Training and Development, 5 Baring Road, Beaconsfield, Bucks HP9 2NX – monthly journal

Video Hire Gower TFI, Gower House, Croft Road, Aldershot, Hants – management training

Christian agencies include:

Church Pastoral Aid Society, Falcon Court, 32 Fleet Street, London EC4Y 1DB

Church of Scotland, A.V. Unit, 22 Colington Road, Edinburgh EH10 5EQ

Scripture Union, Sound and Vision Unit, 130 City Road, London EC1V 2NJ

Voluntary Organizations which offer training courses include:

British Church Growth Association, 59 Warrington Road, Harrow, Middlesex HA1 1SZ – quarterly magazine

National Council for Voluntary Organizations, 26 Bedford Square, London WC1B 3HU

Scripture Union, Training Unit, 9–11 Clothier Road, Bristol BS4 5RL – consultancy, resources and support for those training others in the church

3. *Sources of training exercises*

Much of this material is not designed specifically for church use and may need to be adapted for church-based training.

Annual Handbook for Group Facilitation by Pfeiffer, Jones, Goodstein (University Associates) – yearly publication containing articles, exercises and background information

Communication Games by K. Kruper (Free Press, 1973)

Games Trainers Play (1980) by Newstrom & Scannell (McGraw Hill, 1980)

A Handbook of Management Training Exercises Vols 1 & 2
    ed. J. Adair (BACIE, 1978)
Human Communication Handbook Vols 1 & 2 by B. Ruben
    & R. Budd (Haydon Book Co., 1975)
Learning from Conflict by L. Hart (Addison Wesley,
    1981) – training exercises on handling conflict
Lifeskills Teaching Programmes Vols 1–3 (Lifeskills
    Associates)
Structured Experiences Vols 1–10 ed. J. W. Pfeiffer
    (University Associates, 1973 onwards)

Training in work with children

1. *Books, etc.*

Bringing up Children in the Christian Faith by J. Wes-
    terhoff III (Winston Press, 1980)
The Child in the City by Colin Wood (Architectural
    Press, 1978)
Children Growing Up by Shirley Leslie (Scripture
    Union, 1982)
Children's Minds by M. Donaldson (Fontana, 1978)
Christian Child Development by I. Culley (Gill & Macmil-
    lan, 1979)
Five Plus by P. Dowman (Scripture Union, 1972) –
    looks at 5s–7s
Jesus and the Children by H. R. Weber (World Council of
    Churches, 1979)
Know How to Teach Every Child in Sunday School by D.
    Sherburn (Scripture Union, 1979)
Realities of Childhood by John Inchley (Scripture Union,
    1986)
The Religious Potential of the Child by S. Cavalletti
    (Paulist Press, 1979)
Seven Plus by Margaret Old (Scripture Union, 1972) –
    looks at 7s–10s

Ten Plus by Anton Baumohl (Scripture Union, 1981) – looks at 10s–14s

Using the Bible with All Ages Together by D. L. & P. R. Griggs (Bible Society, 1982)

Using the Bible in Teaching by D. L. Griggs (Bible Society, 1980)

Will Our Children Have Faith? by John Westerhoff III (Seabury Press, 1976)

Working with Children (Scripture Union Training Unit) A D.I.Y. training pack for all working with children

2. *Agencies*

Agencies which offer training and materials include:

Denominational headquarters – children's and education departments

Church Pastoral Aid Society, Falcon Court, 32 Fleet Street, London EC4Y 1DB – CYPECS is their children's section

National Children's Bureau, 8 Wakley Street, London EC1V 7QE

National Christian Education Council, Robert Denholm House, Nutfield, Redhill, Surrey RH1 4HW

Scripture Press, Raans Road, Amersham-on-the-Hill, Bucks HP6 6JQ

Scripture Union, Education in Churches Dept., 130 City Road, London EC1V 2NJ – materials and training

Scripture Union Training Unit, 9–11 Clothier Road, Bristol BS4 5RL – general children's work training

Training in counselling

1. *Books etc.*

Christian Caring D.I.Y. Training Course in Helping Skills – a training course (Scripture Union Training Unit)

Client-centred Therapy by Carl Rogers (Constable, 1965)

Encyclopedia of Psychology ed. D. G. Benner (Marshalls, 1987)

Loss – an invitation to Grow by Jean Grigor (Arthur James, 1986)

Make or Break by Jack Dominion (SPCK, 1984)

Practical Counselling Skills by R. Nelson-Jones (Holt, Rinehart & Winston, 1983)

Restoring the Image by Roger Hurding (Paternoster, 1980)

Roots and Shoots by Roger Hurding (Hodder, 1986)

The Skilled Helper by Egan (Brooks Cole, 1982)

Still Small Voice by Michael Jacobs (SPCK, 1982)

Who Cares? by E. Peterson (Paternoster, 1980)

2. *Agencies*

Higher Education extramural departments of universities, polytechnics, colleges

British Association of Counselling, 37a Sheep Street, Rugby, Warks CV21 3BX

Care and Counsel, St. Mary Magdalen Church, Holloway Road, London N7 8LT – Christian counselling agency involved in training, counselling, research

Clinical Theology Association, St. Mary's House, Church Westcote, Oxford OX7 6SF

Marriage Guidance Council, Herbert Gray College, Little Church Street, Rugby, Warks CV21 3AP

Westminster Pastoral Foundation, St. Marylebone Parish Church, Marylebone Road, London NW1 5LT

Training in evangelism

1. *Books, etc.*

Care to Say Something? (Scripture Union, 1982) – workbook in conversation skills

Out of the Saltshaker by R. M. Pippert (IVP, 1980)

Person to Person (Campus Crusade, Bible Society, Scripture Union) – a ten week training course with video, participants' workbooks and course leader's materials

Share Your Faith (Scripture Union Training Unit) A D.I.Y. training pack in personal evangelism for use by groups in churches

Small Group Evangelism by R. Peace (Scripture Union, 1987)

2. *Agencies*

Denominational agencies – contact headquarters of your denomination for details of courses, materials and advice

Bible Society, Stonehill Green, Westlea, Swindon, Wilts. SN5 7DG

British Youth for Christ, Cleobury Place, Cleobury Mortimer, Kidderminster, Worcs. DY14 8JG

Campus Crusade for Christ, 103 Friar Street, Reading, Berks. RG1 1EP

Evangelism Explosion, 228 Shirley Road, Southampton, Hants. SO1 3HR

Scripture Union, Missions Dept., 130 City Road, London EC1V 2NJ

Scripture Union, Schools Dept., 130 City Road, London EC1V 2NJ

Scripture Union Training Unit, 9–11 Clothier Road, Bristol BS4 5RL

Training in work with the family

1. *Books, etc.*

Christians in Families by R. T. Bender (Herald, 1982)

Families in Britain ed. Rapoport, Fogarty & Rapoport (RKP, 1982)

Know How to Encourage Family Worship by Howard Mellor (Scripture Union, 1984)

Know How – All Age Activities for Learning and Worship by Michael Lush (Scripture Union, 1983)

Making Time for the Family (Scripture Union Training Unit) – a training pack for use in the local church on various topics in family ministry

On Being Family by R. S. Anderson and D. B. Guernsey (Eerdmans, 1986) – a social theology of the family

Open University Community Education Series (reference numbers P593, P596, P597, P598, P912) – various parenting modules

Side by Side (CPAS) – marriage preparation course with video

2. *Agencies*

CLASP (Christian Link Association of Single Parents), Linden Shorter Avenue, Shenfield, Brentwood CM15 8RE – produce training materials

Family Base, Jubilee Centre, 3 Hooper Street, Cambridge CB1 2NZ

Family Life Education Ecumenical Project, Church and Society Dept., United Reformed Church, 86 Tavistock Place, London WC1H 9RT

Marriage Encounter (Anglican), 4 Hall Place Gardens, St. Albans, Herts AL1 3SP

Marriage Encounter (Baptist), 12 South Street, Leighton Buzzard, Beds. LU7 8NT

National Marriage Guidance Council

Scripture Union, Family Adviser, 130 City Road, London EC1V 2NJ

Training in management

1. *Books etc.*

Seconds Away by David Cormack (Marc Europe, 1986)

So You Think You Can Manage by Video Arts (Methuen, 1984)

Team Spirit by D. Cormack (Marc Europe, 1987)

Up the Organisation by R. Townsend (Coronet, 1970)

Yes Manager – Management in the local church by Brian Pearson (Grove Books, 1986)

2. *Agencies*

Administry, 69 Sandridge Road, St. Albans, Herts AL1 4AG – run courses, publish papers and resources

Gower TFI, Gower House, Croft Road, Aldershot, Hants GU11 3HR – produce good management training videos

MAAZTEC (Europe) Ltd., Strathurdle House, Enochdhu, Perthshire PH10 7PB – courses in management

Marc Europe, Cosmos House, 6 Homesdale Road, Bromley, Kent BR2 9EX – run courses, publish books

Time Manager International – courses and material on time management

Video Arts, Dunbarton House, 68 Oxford Street, London W1N 9LA – produce good management training videos

Westhill College, Wesley Park Road, Selly Oak, Birmingham B29 6LL – run courses in management through their church education programme

Training for small group leadership

1. *Books, etc.*

Building Small Groups in the Christian Community by John Mallison (Scripture Union, 1978)

Creative Ideas for Small Groups by John Mallison (Scripture Union, 1978)

Good Things Come in Small Groups (Scripture Union, 1987)

Joining Together by Johnson & Johnson (Prentice Hall, 1982) – excellent training manual on small group leadership

Leading Groups – a training course by M. Parker (Epworth, 1978)

Leading Small Groups (Scripture Union Training Unit) – a D.I.Y. training pack for all who lead small groups

Learning to Work in Groups by M. B. Miles (Teachers College Press, 1981)

Once Upon a Group by M. Kindred (Southwell Diocese Education Committee, 1984)

Red Book of Groups by G. Houston (Rochester Foundation, 1984)

Serendipity Leader's Manual by Lyman Coleman (Scripture Union) – contains a six session training course

Using the Bible in Groups by R. Hestenes (Bible Society, 1983)

Working in Groups – workbook and video. Workbook produced by TACADE, video distributed by Concord Films

2. *Agencies*

Denominational agencies

Bible Society, Stonehill Green, Westlea, Swindon, Wiltshire, SN5 7DG

Church Pastoral Aid Society, Falcon Court, 32 Fleet Street, London EC4Y 1DB produce a magazine for house group leaders

Group Relations Training Associations – material and regional courses on groups. Write to Hugh Lennon, 12 Fabian Road, London SW6

Grubb Institute, Cloudesley Street, London N1 0HV

Regional Churches Training Groups, Church House, Deans Yard, London SW1P 3NZ

Scripture Union Training Unit, 9–11 Clothier Road, Bristol BS4 5RL – run courses in all aspects of small group work

Serendipity UK, 48 Peterborough Road, London SW6 3EB – run courses for small groups

Surrey University, Department of Educational Studies, University of Surrey, Guildford GU2 5XH

Training for urban ministry

1. *Books, etc.*

Bias to the Poor by D. Sheppard (Hodder and Stoughton, 1984)

Built as a City by D. Sheppard (Hodder and Stoughton, 1974)

ECUM Resource Book for Urban Ministry

Jesus Is Your Best Mate by D. Cave (Marshalls, 1985)

Poverty, Revolution and the Church by M. Paget-Wilkes (Paternoster, 1981)

Signs in the City by Colin Marchant (Hodder, 1985)

The Urban Christian by R. Bakke (Marc Europe, 1987)

Urban Harvest by R. Joslin (Evangelical Press, 1982)

2. *Agencies*

Evangelical Coalition for Urban Mission, Scripture Union House, 130 City Road, London EC1V 2NJ

Evangelical Urban Training Project, PO Box 83,
   Liverpool, Merseyside L69 8AN
Urban Theology Unit, Pitsmoor Study House, 210
   Abbeyfield Road, Sheffield, S. Yorks. S4 7AZ

Leading Worship

1. *Books etc.*

Know How to Use Art in Worship by Valerie Bennett
   (Scripture Union, 1985)
Know How to Use Dance in Worship by Madeleine Berry
   (Scripture Union, 1985)
One Heart, One Voice by A. Maries (Hodder, 1986)
Ten Worshipping Churches ed. G. Kendrick (Marc
   Europe, 1987)
Worship by Graham Kendrick (Kingsway, 1984)

2. *Agencies*

Kingsway Publishers, Lottbridge Drove, Eastbourne,
   E. Sussex BN23 6NT – run worship courses
Lamplugh House, Thwing, Driffield, N. Humberside
   YO25 0DY – run courses

Training in youth work

1. *Books, etc.*

Christian Youth Work by M. Ashton (Kingsway Publica-
   tions, 1987)
Inside Out ed M. Eastman (Frontier Youth Trust, 1976)
Mission and Young People at Risk by Terry Dunnell
   (Frontier Youth Trust, 1985)
Six Training Sessions for your Youthworker Team by
   Lyman Coleman (Scripture Union, 1983)
Starting from Strengths (NYB) – looks at the training of
   volunteers

Using the Bible with Youth by D. Halls (Bible Society, 1981)

Youth in Society – monthly journal from National Youth Bureau

Youth Leadership (Scripture Union Training Unit) – a D.I.Y. training pack for all working with young people

2. *Agencies*

Denominational agencies – all have youth departments

Uniformed organizations – organize training for affiliated groups

British Youth for Christ, Cleobury Place, Cleobury Mortimer, Kidderminster, Worcs. DY14 8JG – resources

Church Pastoral Aid Society (CYFA), Falcon Court, 32 Fleet Street, London EC4Y 1DB – materials and courses

Frontier Youth Trust, 130 City Road, London EC1V 2NJ – publications, courses, support and advice

National Association of Youth Clubs, Keswick House, 30 Peacock Lane, Leicester LE1 5NY

National Council for Voluntary Youth Service (NCVYS), Wellington House, 29 Albion Street, Leicester LE1 6JG – courses and materials

National Youth Bureau, 17–23 Albion Street, Leicester LE1 6GD – publications and research

Scripture Union, Schools Dept., 130 City Road, London EC1V 2NJ

Scripture Union, Training Unit, 9–11 Clothier Road, Bristol BS4 5RL

Serendipity UK, 48 Peterborough Road, London SW6 3EB – courses in using the Bible with young people

THINGS TO DO

1. Survey all the training resources available in your church. If possible, bring them together and group them in the most helpful way.
2. Looking at the areas of ministry in your church, what gaps are there in your resources? Identify and then discover what is available to fill these gaps.

9
Developing a
Training Strategy

Offering the occasional training course for leaders, to
meet their immediate needs, or setting up a regular
apprenticeship scheme, will go some way to equipping individuals for the work to which God has called
them. Developing a *strategy* for the church's training
will take this a stage further by building training more
fully into the life and mission of the church.

The word 'strategy' describes a thought-through,
co-ordinated approach. To have a training strategy in
the local church means developing approaches and
programmes for training in the various areas of church
life – not simply as a means of maintaining the status
quo of the various church organizations but in a desire
to see God's people equipped for his mission, and as
one element of their discipleship. So far we have
concentrated our exploration of training on the *micro*
level – ie the specifics of various methods and areas of
training. As we consider strategy, we must step back
for a more distant and all-embracing view, looking at
the way training affects the whole church in the long
term.

When developing a strategy we can either plan for
the local church as a whole, with all its activities, teams

and leaders, or we can focus on just one area of church life. The rest of this chapter can be related to either level.

A strategy requires the following elements:

1. The development of training programmes for the relevant area(s) of ministry in the church so that training and support are regularly on offer to potential leaders, new leaders and experienced leaders.
2. Space in the church's diary when training activities can take place.
3. Resources – materials, people and money set aside for training for ministry.
4. A regular review of the training activities of the church, so that it is kept relevant to the needs in the church and remains fresh and vital.

The flow chart below takes us back through the material in this book in order to create a logical sequence for planning a strategy.

1. *Starting small*

If your resources and time are limited, be prepared to start small! Look at the areas in the church where training would be more readily acceptable and where implementation wouldn't be too much of a problem. Try some of the following:

a) Use existing meetings of leaders, if they occur, as the place to introduce some training (the monthly Sunday school teachers' meeting, the half-yearly meeting of the house group leaders, etc).

b) Buy a flexible training package and use selected material to resource the training, or invite someone in from outside to take a training session.

c) Find someone in the group who will take responsibility for training in that group by either collecting

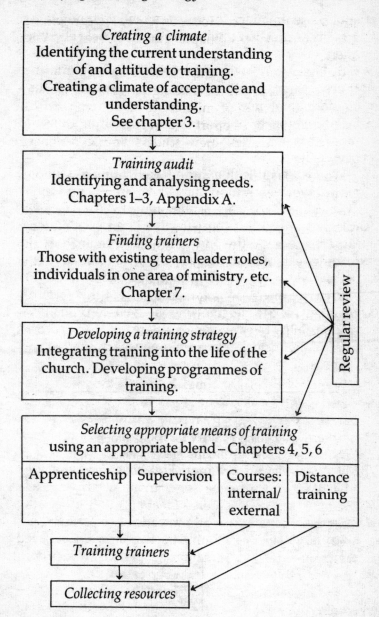

Creating a climate
Identifying the current understanding
of and attitude to training.
Creating a climate of acceptance and
understanding.
See chapter 3.

Training audit
Identifying and analysing needs.
Chapters 1–3, Appendix A.

Finding trainers
Those with existing team leader roles,
individuals in one area of ministry, etc.
Chapter 7.

Developing a training strategy
Integrating training into the life of the
church. Developing programmes of
training.

Regular review

Selecting appropriate means of training
using an appropriate blend – Chapters 4, 5, 6

Apprenticeship	Supervision	Courses: internal/ external	Distance training

Training trainers

Collecting resources

and disseminating information about training or actually seeing that training sessions are held every so often.

d) Begin to introduce the idea of training into the church through other events – house group discussion, sermons.

e) Move on to other groups in the church once a model has been established and some experience has been gained.

Where it is difficult to introduce training to a whole group, work with individuals who are open to their own training – perhaps as they agree to take on a new role or want to be more effective in an existing job. Supervise the individual using a combination of reading, external courses and distance training packages. Two or three individuals in different areas of church life might be prepared to accept this form of training. Next time someone is given co-ordinating responsibility over a team or an area of church work discuss the inclusion of a training role in their job.

CASE STUDY 24:
A training strategy for house groups

A church has six house groups which meet twice monthly for Bible study, prayer and support. Each house group has two leaders

Training	Target groups	Purpose	Frequency/ Duration
Sampler Course	New leaders, potential leaders, anyone who wants to know more	To give an introduction to house group leadership. To provide enough basic training for a new leader	One whole day every two years

Training	Target groups	Purpose	Frequency/ Duration
Apprenticeship	People preparing to take on a group. Church attempts to anticipate leadership changes well in advance	To provide on-the-job training of new leaders before they take sole responsibility for a group of their own	Eight house group sessions plus eight review sessions
Distance training	When a sudden change in leadership is necessary	To provide basic emergency training for individuals	Guided reading and chats with trainer at own convenience
Supervision	Existing leaders	Mutual support and supervision of each other at team meeting	At regular house group leaders' meetings: once a month for 2½ hours in an evening
Ongoing training	Existing leaders	A syllabus of four topics drawn up each year, covering areas identified by the leaders with space for adding new training needs as they arise	1½ hour slot given at every other leaders' meeting. If a major topic arises, extra time is given on Saturday

Trainer: One member of the house group team acts as trainer. This involves keeping the scheme going, having access to distance training materials, spending time preparing those leaders who will take on apprentices, etc.

2. *Starting big*

A concerted effort to introduce training as a ministry in a local church could be developed using a combination of the following:

a) Holding a teaching and preaching series on the place of training, service, use of gifts, etc. in the life of the church.

b) Conducting a training audit in the church.

c) Appointing trainer(s) and training them for their

role – either giving existing team leaders a training responsibility, or inviting those with a gift for training to take on a specialist training ministry in the church.

d) Developing a resource library to support the trainers.

CASE STUDY 25:
A training strategy for a church

The church has identified areas of church life where training is offered for those with responsibility.

Sectional training	Under the leadership of people responsible for putting together training programmes, each area of ministry plans its own regular training needs, spread over one, two or three years. These are carried out within each section using a variety of means and resources.
Co-ordinated training	Once a year those with training responsibility in different areas of ministry meet together to outline the training plans and needs of their group. Any training needs or plans common to more than one area of ministry are considered for some form of combined training.
Sample training	Every two years a sampler day is organized. Each area of ministry offers a half-day training programme to give interested/potential leaders a taste of what they do. On that day people have the chance to taste up to two areas of ministry. This is one means by which the church looks for new leaders.

Trainer: The church has a training co-ordinator who oversees all training in the church. He/she delegates much to those with a training responsibility in their area of ministry. The co-ordinator provides support when it is needed for those sections of the church having their own trainer. The co-ordinator is more heavily involved in those areas of church life which do not have a trainer, areas involving a small number of people, or 'temporary' activities requiring short-term leadership.

The co-ordinator resources other trainers *and* initiates and supports new training schemes.

THINGS TO DO

1. Develop a strategy for your church or section of the church. Start by listing the:
     i) people and their needs
    ii) different means of training that could be used
   iii) time available for training
   iv) resources available (including people as re-sources)
2. Now try to put these together into a year planner ensuring that there is regular training and support for:
     i) newcomers and potential leaders
    ii) the experienced.

Appendix A
Training Audit

The purpose of this audit is to help churches to begin to plan for training. It can be used to plan training for *one section* of the church's work (eg youth work, evangelism) or to prepare an overall strategy for training in *all areas* of church work. It can be completed by an individual or a small group.

1. IDENTIFY THE JOBS/TASKS/MINISTRIES/ ROLES IN THE CHURCH

List all the jobs/tasks/ministries/roles in your church – both permanent and temporary (see p. 55 for ideas).

Indicate by each the level of training you feel they demand: Write D by any that you feel require long-term developmental training (eg children's workers, pastoral team members); S by any that require short-term, limited training (eg catering team members); and O by any that require simple one-off training (eg houseparty organizer). Add an E beside any job that requires some existing experience or qualification (eg mini-bus driver, electrician).

2. IDENTIFY JOB REQUIREMENTS

Fill in this analysis form for any job for which you wish to plan training (see chapter 3). Star any items that you consider to be essential – these become the priorities when planning training.

Name of job/task/ministry/role:		
Knowledge required	Attitudes/values required	Skills required

3. JOB DESCRIPTION

Use the outline below to write a job description, as a means of communicating the nature of the job to someone about to take it on.

Title:

Responsible to:

Responsible for:

Working relationships with:

Nature and purpose of job:

Major tasks:
1.
2.
3.
4.
5.
6.
7.
8.
9.
10.

4. SKILLS ANALYSIS

List all the skills needed to do the job – Appendix B
may help you.

Job/role etc.

a) *Communication skills:*
   All those skills that enable
   people to communicate with a
   large group, small group or even
   one to one, eg using drama,
   OHP, giving an illustrated talk,
   leading a discussion group.

b) *Human relations skills:*
   All those skills that help people
   in their relationships with
   others, eg developing self-
   awareness, becoming sensitive
   to others, listening, developing
   trust and openness, building
   friendships with children and
   teenagers, handling conflict, etc.

c) *Organization skills:*
   eg preparing a teaching
   programme, organizing games,
   planning budgets, preparing a
   committee agenda.

d) *Mechanical skills:*
   eg working a computer, an OHP,
   a duplicator, filmstrip projector,
   playing games and sports.

5. IDENTIFY SPECIAL TRAINING NEEDS

Identify needs that are specific to the group or individual being trained, or to the situation in which they are working (see chapter 3 for more details). This analysis can be used when trying to identify the training needs of more experienced leaders.

	Special needs of those involved in training	Special needs created by the situation or locality
Identified by those *participating* in training		
Identified by the *trainer*		

Appendix B

Skills Checklist

A checklist of skills is provided for some major areas of churchwork. If you are not used to viewing ministry in terms of skills these lists should act as a catalyst. The lists are not meant to be exhaustive – do identify and add others. The symbols used are as follows: C = communication skills; H = human relations skills; O = organizational skills; M = mechanical skills.

Pastoral carer
listening (CH)
questioning (C)
clarifying (C)
paraphrasing (C)
reflecting emotions (CH)
confronting (H)
problem-solving (HO)
decision-making (HO)
sensitive to non-verbal
  messages (H)
personal awareness (H)
inter-personal
  communication (HC)
creating a secure
  atmosphere (H)

Committee chairperson
setting an agenda (O)
initiating discussion (C)
problem-solving
  methods (CO)
decision-making
  methods (CO)
facilitating a discussion
  (C)
handling conflict (H)
handling people's
  emotions (H)
sensitivity to process in
  small groups (H)

Youth leader
listening (CH)
building relationships (H)
using AVA equipment (M)
handling finances (O)
organizing games (O)
programme planning (O)
first aid (M)
giving a short talk (C)
handling disruptive behaviour (H)
leading a discussion (C)
working in a team (H)
use of a variety of techniques for learning (C)
playing games (M)

Worship leader
leading a large group (CO)
use of voice (C)
sensitivity to groups and mood (H)
variety of working techniques (C)
musical skills (M)
conducting skills (M)
programme planning (O)
controlling and changing pace (CO)
awareness of self (H)

House group leader
listening (CH)
programme planning (O)
leading a Bible study (C)
leading a discussion (C)
handling people's emotions (H)
facilitating a group (HC)
using AVA equipment (M)
counselling skills (HC)
sensitive to non-verbal messages (H)
personal awareness (H)
creating an appropriate atmosphere (H)
use of a variety of techniques (C)

Trainer
listening (CH)
facilitating (C)
programme planning (O)
course design (O)
a variety of techniques (C)
evaluation (O)
giving and receiving feedback (CH)
counselling skills (CH)
personal awareness (H)
sensitivity to others (H)
using AVA equipment (M)
building relationships (H)

Sunday school teacher
listening (CH)
using drama with
    children (H)
planning a programme
    (O)
using AVA equipment
    (M)
making and using visual
    aids (MC)
building relationships
    with children (H)
handling disruptive
    behaviour (H)
using activity methods
    (C)
counselling children
    (HC)
telling a story (C)
encouraging children to
    talk (C)
using games for learning
    (C)
playing a musical
    instrument (M)
leading worship (OC)

Teacher/preacher
use of voice (C)
structuring a talk (O)
use of AVA equipment
    (M)
preparation and use of
    visual aids (MC)

handling questions in a
    large group (C)
use of techniques to help
    people reflect and
    apply (CH)
using a variety of
    resources in
    preparation (O)
use of hands and body
    (C)
personal awareness (eg
    mannerisms) (H)
methods of varying
    presentation (CO)

Treasurer
preparing a budget (O)
presenting accounts (OC)
book keeping (O)

Missionary secretary
programme planning (O)
leading a small group
    (CH)
variety of teaching/
    learning techniques (C)
poster design/production
    (OM)
wall displays (OM)
producing newsletters
    (OC)
motivation skills (CH)

Lesson reader
use of voice (C)
posture (M)
breathing (M)

Magazine editor
design and layout (O)
print processes (M)
editing (OC)
journalistic skills (C)
dry transfer lettering (M)
use of illustrations (O)

Some skills are common to different areas of work. This could indicate a need for a form of training that focuses on a skill or issue which is relevant to people from a variety of areas of church work, and to which they could all be invited, e.g:

• A course on basic listening skills could be open to anyone in the church.

• A course on using the overhead projector could be offered to house group leaders, youth workers, children's workers and preachers.

Appendix C
Sample Training Course Outlines

COURSE OUTLINES

The course outlines below illustrate how objectives, training subjects, methods and timings can be brought together. The annotations represent the trainer's explanation of the design. These examples are not given as 'packages' for churches to take and use – they would need to be adapted to their own needs and situations.

1. An evening course (2 hours) for the welcoming team – some new, some experienced.

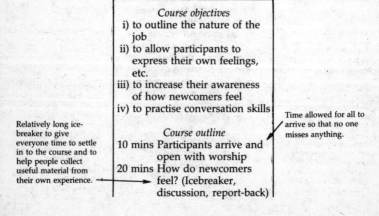

Course objectives

i) to outline the nature of the job

ii) to allow participants to express their own feelings, etc.

iii) to increase their awareness of how newcomers feel

iv) to practise conversation skills

Course outline

10 mins Participants arrive and open with worship

20 mins How do newcomers feel? (Icebreaker, discussion, report-back)

Relatively long ice-breaker to give everyone time to settle in to the course and to help people collect useful material from their own experience.

Time allowed for all to arrive so that no one misses anything.

Trainer acts as builder, helping people to see the nature of the job and its context in the church. (Could give out job descriptions here.)

Allows people to talk about their experiences in the role play, to identify problems they still have and gives trainer the opportunity to see if more training is required.

30 mins How do welcomers feel? (Pairs sharing and large group discussion)

15 mins The nature of the job (illustrated talk)

35 mins Conversation skills practice (role play in pairs)

10 mins Questions and coffee
A handout covering procedures and some principles is given out at the end of the course

This feeds off the ice-breaker and allows other ideas to be introduced by the trainer if necessary.

Practising a basic skill. An exercise is introduced by trainer: in pairs one takes role of welcomer, the other a 'type' of newcomer.

2. A half-day course (3¼ hours) for the pastoral team – all with some experience.

Course objectives
i) to explore how people communicate their feelings
ii) to examine how participants handle their own and others' feelings when counselling

Course outline

Structured exercise that encourages people to identify feelings being expressed (usually non-verbally) by others.

Trainer acting as builder, providing a theoretical framework to help people in their understanding.

The most sensitive part of the programme. Individuals use a questionnaire-style handout to identify how they react to and handle feelings in others. Group sharing and time spent in identifying areas where individuals would like to do some work.

15 mins How do you feel? Opening exercise in pairs with discussion

45 mins Expressing and identifying feelings (human relations exercise and discussion)

25 mins Observing non-verbal behaviour (video of a TV soap opera)

15 mins Non-verbal behaviour (illustrated talk)

30 mins Sharing experiences (small groups)

45 mins Handling feelings (personal inventory and group sharing)

20 mins Questions, closing devotions and refreshments

Getting people to reflect on their own immediate feelings and to get used to putting feelings into words.

Reinforcing the last exercise, the video being shown without the sound.

A chance for people to draw on their past experiences and to learn from others' experience. The course is kept together by having a brief report-back of the major points raised in each group.

Trainer gauges possible future training for individuals or group.

3. A day course (6 hours) on teamwork for the youth leaders – a mix of experienced and new leaders all with some past training or experience.

Course objectives

i) to develop closer relations between a group of youth leaders

ii) to explore the meaning of teamwork

iii) to develop skills of working as a team

Course outline

15 mins Coffee

30 mins Story sharing in twos and fours

20 mins What makes a team? (Small group discussion)

30 mins Developing trust (Human relations exercise)

20 mins The values and dangers of openness and honesty (Small group discussion)

45 mins Meal break

50 mins Handling conflict (Human relations exercise)

40 mins The place of affirmation (Human relations exercise)

30 mins Tea break

60 mins Teamwork practical (Human relations exercise)

20 mins Summary (Questions and conclusions)

Display of a range of books and materials available

Uses people's experience to provide definitions and some theoretical framework. The trainer adds other ideas during report-back from groups. Ideas recorded on a flipchart.

Another element of teamwork is explored through discussion in same fours. Some guidelines drawn up from the combined groups' conclusions.

Fourth element of teamwork. The fours actually learn to affirm one another.

Trainer asks the question: 'What have you learned today?' After personal reflection, individuals share with others and pray for one another in their fours.

Icebreaker is geared to build people into small groups of four that will become their team for the duration of this course.

Provides an *experience* of one element of teamwork aimed at bringing the fours closer together. This takes up one element of teamwork identified in the last exercise. Short discussion on how trust develops in a team.

Fours eat together.

Third element of teamwork is again explored experientially – involvement vital after lunch break as people are often sleepy.

Fours given a task to complete in period of time. After completion, fours are asked to look at the way they worked together, how individuals felt and the roles people played.

4. A specialist workshop (3 hours) in the use of drama for all those working with children and teenagers.

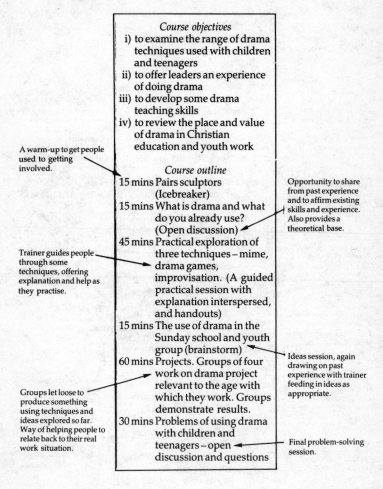

Course objectives

i) to examine the range of drama techniques used with children and teenagers

ii) to offer leaders an experience of doing drama

iii) to develop some drama teaching skills

iv) to review the place and value of drama in Christian education and youth work

Course outline

15 mins Pairs sculptors (Icebreaker)

15 mins What is drama and what do you already use? (Open discussion)

45 mins Practical exploration of three techniques – mime, drama games, improvisation. (A guided practical session with explanation interspersed, and handouts)

15 mins The use of drama in the Sunday school and youth group (brainstorm)

60 mins Projects. Groups of four work on drama project relevant to the age with which they work. Groups demonstrate results.

30 mins Problems of using drama with children and teenagers – open discussion and questions

A warm-up to get people used to getting involved.

Opportunity to share from past experience and to affirm existing skills and experience. Also provides a theoretical base.

Trainer guides people through some techniques, offering explanation and help as they practise.

Ideas session, again drawing on past experience with trainer feeding in ideas as appropriate.

Groups let loose to produce something using techniques and ideas explored so far. Way of helping people to relate back to their real work situation.

Final problem-solving session.

5. An evening course (1¾ hours) on developing listening skills. Designed for anyone involved in working with others (children/youth workers;

pastoral team members; visitors, pensioners' group leaders, committee members, elders, deacons, ministers, trainers, etc.).

Course objectives

i) to make people aware of the meaning of the term 'listening'

ii) to help people to become better listeners

iii) to help people apply listening skills to their work

Course outline

10 mins Meet and talk with someone not too well known to you (Icebreaker)

Icebreaker but with hidden purpose of providing a listening experience.

Using icebreaker as an experience of good or bad listening helps to drive home the point, that listening isn't easy.

15 mins How well did you listen? Pairs link with second pairs and introduce their partner

10 mins What is real listening and why is it important? (Illustrated talk)

Theoretical framework.

30 mins Practising listening (Human relations, listening exercises in pairs)

Using experience of last exercise and past experience to produce a useful list.

Two or three short exercises that help people to practise the skill of listening.

15 mins What aids and hinders our listening? (Open discussion)

15 mins In what ways is listening important in our church work and how do you need to improve? (Individual reflection and writing, shared in pairs)

Encouraging people to relate to their own work situation and to think of practical outworkings of this course.

10 mins Concluding questions and time of silent meditation, listening to God

Handout covering some main points given out as people leave

Opportunity for questions and closing worship that continues the theme of the evening.